# WRITING
## TO
## READ

# WRITING
# TO
# READ

**A Parents' Guide to the New, Early Learning
Program for Young Children**

## Dr. John Henry Martin
## and
## Ardy Friedberg

**WARNER BOOKS**

A Warner Communications Company

A Warner Communications Company

Printed in the United States of America
First Printing: January 1986
10  9  8  7  6  5  4  3  2  1


**Library of Congress Cataloging in Publication Data**

Martin, John Henry, 1915–
  Writing to read.

  1. Reading (Primary)—Computer-assisted instruction.
2. English language—Composition and exercises—
Computer-assisted instruction.   3. Learning centers.
I. Friedberg, Ardy.  II. Title.
LB1525.4.M37  1986      649′.58      85-26347
ISBN 0-446-51341-5

Dedicated to
*Evelyn Martin*

# CONTENTS

# ACKNOWLEDGMENTS

This book is made possible only by the generosity of the International Business Machines Corporation, which has given permission to use large extracts from materials which I authored originally and on which they now own the copyright.

Part of the generosity and statesmanship of the IBM Corporation can be measured by the fact that they were the only computer hardware company or publisher that was willing to accept our insistence that the Writing to Read System not be sold to the school systems of America until our research in the development of the materials, which had involved nearly 1,000 children over five years, was further subjected to a large-scale national test involving some 10,000 children. IBM financed this study by providing in excess of 300 computers, 600 typewriters, tape recorders, earphones, large quantities of work materials, and the diskettes for the computerized program. In addition, they employed an outside evaluator, the Educational Testing Service of Princeton, New Jersey, to measure the consequences of the test, and only when the results proved significantly superior to conventional alternative methods of teaching reading did they go ahead and market their product.

More than a few publishing houses were eager to buy the Writing to Read System and to go immediately into publication and sales. Only IBM saw the wisdom and need to protect the children of America from computer products and procedures that were experimental and largely untested. They subjected the Writing to Read System to rigorous field testing in 1982, then extended their commitment for an additional year while the Educational Testing Service confirmed, in a study of 10,000 children, that the results indicated that this method of teaching writing and reading to kindergarten and first grade children was superior to a degree not matched by any other system.

For all of this, we express our prideful acknowledgment and thanks.

It's usual in this section for authors to give credit to people who have contributed to their thinking and whose previous research has served as the basis for their own. In addition to the research of Piaget, Skinner, Bruner, Orton, the Spaldings, and others, we would like to give credit to Alvin C. Eurich, who gave encouragement and support during the early years of our research, and also to acknowledge a lifelong dependence on a giant in the history of American education and the psychology of learning, Ben Wood. This exceptional man, entering his ninety-first year as this is written, has been a lifelong friend, a lifelong mentor, and a pioneer in the use of technology to improve the education of children.

Thousands of children participated in the experimental stages of Writing to Read, and their work was an inspiration to us, to the staff of JHM Corporation who helped support the field program, and to their teachers and parents. Included in this book are many representative pieces of writing from the countless stories written by those children and to all of them we are indebted. And while we want to thank all the teachers and administrators who helped compile this material, we want to give special thanks to the administrators and the staff of the Washington, D.C., public schools. We have used a number of the stories from their school district, because they show how the program develops writing skills.

Also a note of special thanks to Dr. William Turnbull, friend and scholar, who worked with us in the early evaluation of *Writing to Read* before the more extensive nationwide study by the Educational Testing Service. Because we value the findings of that report, we have summarized sections of it in several parts of this book.

*—JHM*

# INTRODUCTION

Crystal ī love you. that diamn ī gav you wuz not rēl.

bobby

I have a cat. He is silly. He likes to play with string. He allways comes to sleep with me. Evry night, befoor he goes to sleep he comes up to my pillow and claws.

Kristian

One da mī mommy wok me up and ī got drest and ī at brafist. mī mommy took me to thu toi stor and ī had ten dolers and ī but a bābē doll.

heather

BOBBY, KRISTIAN, and Heather were all kindergartners when they wrote these short little stories. They used a computer to write them but they could have used a typewriter or a pencil and paper just as easily. At the time, Bobby and his friends, all average students in an average class in the mill town of Burlington, North Carolina, had been involved for only three and a half months in the then revolutionary educational experiment known as Writing to Read.*

Are the accomplishments of these average children out of the ordinary? Yes, indeed.

Don't all kindergartners write sentences like this? They certainly do not. In fact most kindergartners never have the opportunity to write anything but the alphabet.

Did they learn quickly? Yes, three and a half months is a short time to learn to write.

---

*Writing to Read is a Trademark of IBM Corporation.

What is just as surprising is that Bobby, Kristian, Heather, and most of their classmates were able to write their words, sentences, and stories even though they had not yet begun their school's formal reading curriculum, a part of the instructional cycle that doesn't start until the middle of the first grade. Traditionally, in American schools, children are taught to read before they can write, and the sentences and stories written by these Burlington children are not normally seen from even bright students until they are in the final days of first grade, by which time the majority are seven years old.

It's also important to keep in mind that these were not isolated cases from a bright class in a select school. Thousands of other children in all parts of the country participated in the Writing to Read program and turned out this same high-level work on a daily basis.

I developed the Writing to Read System after a lifelong study of how children begin the process of learning to read and write. It is an innovative concept not only in that it teaches children to write before they are able to read, or that they do this writing at such an early age, or even that they are taught to use a typewriter and a computer from the very first day, but because Writing to Read teaches a child how to convert the sounds he or she already knows how to speak into "sounds" that can be written down.

The teaching methodology embodied in Writing to Read allows the child to write at the upper levels of his or her ability to think and talk, and to perform this complicated task with a high degree of proficiency in a matter of only a few weeks or months.

In 1983 and 1984 Writing to Read was tested in 105 schools in twenty-two school systems (city, suburban, and rural) across the country. More than 10,000 five- and six-year-old children participated. This experimental group came from families that represented all economic levels and ethnic groups. The Educational Testing Service (ETS) in Princeton, New Jersey, evaluated the program using a combination of the individual school districts' standard achievement tests and a series of other evaluation techniques, including opinion and attitude surveys of parents and teachers. In the districts that tested children at the end of the first year with the standard California Achievement Test, the findings are strikingly consistent. They show that the children in Writing to Read scored higher in reading skills than 89 percent of their peers. On completing kindergarten, 63 percent of the program participants were composing and typing full, original sentences and stories. Joshua, one of these kindergarten children, wrote:

> Once there livd an old woman and an old man and they livd in a kōsey littel house. And they had ten galons of milk and they ate lots of chees. They wer pritty comfrtible with all the stuff they had.

This kind of performance is unusual because national statistics show that fewer than 25 percent of all children can write their names in kindergarten. Yet the majority of kindergarten children in Writing to Read write as well as Joshua. In the first grade, 92 percent of the children in Writing to Read were writing stories like Joshua's as well as reading at levels higher than anticipated for their age. And equally as important, these results were achieved regardless of geography, the child's family background, race, or economic status. In other words, the program worked for a very high percentage of all children. Second-year test results from the school districts showed the same dramatic achievements as those found at the end of the first year.

It should be emphasized that it's rare when educational research and experimentation such as this is conducted on a broad scale. Most test programs are initiated in a handful of classes in one school and then the results are extrapolated to show what it would mean if the program was adopted on a limited basis in a few schools in a single school district. A study that involves more than 200 children is considered large. Not so with Writing to Read. The sample we tested is broad enough and deep enough to have nationwide implications, and the proof is that Writing to Read is now being adopted in school districts across the country. Following the release of the ETS report in July 1984, IBM Corporation announced that the Writing to Read System would be mar-

keted to the schools, and in five months, more than 100,000
children were learning with the system.

The ETS evaluation included classroom observation of
the way Writing to Read functions, interviews and ques-
tionnaires for teachers and parents, and the design of eval-
uative tools for testing writing and spelling skills. In the
second year the study focused on a national core sample of
3,210 students who used the program and 2,379 who did
not use it. ETS used rigorous techniques of group comparison, before-and-after testing, and statistical analysis to sort
out the effects of the program. The major findings show that
children learn with Writing to Read:

- *In Reading:* Standardized reading tests showed
  that kindergarten and first grade Writing to Read
  students, on the average, progressed faster than
  the national norm samples.

  On the same standardized tests, Writing to
  Read students in kindergarten demonstrated a
  significant advantage over comparison kindergarten students in reading ability; the average
  advantage was 15 percentile points.

- *In Writing:* By the end of the program, 72 percent
  of the students in Writing to Read had progressed beyond word-level writing to the writing
  of phrases and sentences, and in 15 percent of
  the cases to more developed writing that is considerably above normal expectations for children
  at that level.

- *In Spelling:* Writing to Read students performed
  at slightly higher levels than comparison groups
  in spelling.

ETS found that teachers responded to the program in
much the same way as Daytona Beach, Florida, Volusia
County School Superintendent Dr. James Surratt, who said:
"This is the first time in a long time that I've seen schools
give a child something that was the most exciting thing in

his life." Teachers reported observing greater progress by their students in reading and writing, and they indicated that because of the success of the program they felt like spending more time on writing and reading than in previous years. Parents told ETS that their children liked Writing to Read and that they saw a good deal of evidence of reading and writing skills at home, and 93 percent of the parents said they hoped their school would continue using the program.

Is Writing to Read the wave of the educational future? Is it a method of teaching that can be used in any school system? Is it a way parents can teach their children to write and read at home? I think the answer to all these questions is yes, and I think you'll agree with me after you've read the following chapters. We are extremely pleased by the evolution and performance of Writing to Read, and we are glad that we can share it with parents.

*—JHM*

# WRITING
# TO
# READ

# CHAPTER 1

# THE NATURE OF THIS BOOK

> Today Miss Dow is teching us. I like her. When I growup I want to be a techer. I wish I could be rich or butiful.

WRITING TO READ teaches kindergarten children to write with the skill shown by the author of this testimony to Miss Dow. Writing to Read teaches children to read by teaching them to write. This book describes that process in detail from two perspectives—the school and the home. The first chapters will give you a complete description of Writing to Read as the program operates in the schools. Throughout this section you will find a good deal of information on the research bases and the historical sources used in the development of the program. As you read this description, you will not only begin to understand what Writing to Read does and what it teaches children to do, but you will be absorbing its major components and ideas, which will enable you to apply the principles of the program at home.

From time to time, we have included explanations and commentaries on why we emphasize certain aspects of learning that are either unknown to the schools, are known but have been neglected by the schools over the last five decades, or were used for a time and then dropped by the schools for one reason or another. These comments are not meant to deride previous or current efforts to innovate in public education but to point out how Writing to Read capitalized on the best of those efforts and how we attempted to avoid the pitfalls of those programs that proved to be less than successful.

We have also spent a good deal of time explaining how Writing to Read works with the computer because the system was developed with the computer in mind. The instructional diskettes that are the heart of the computer program are currently available only to school systems, but we have worked successfully without high technology, using the same principles on which those diskettes were developed. In our research and development we used pencil and paper and the typewriter before we used the computer, and the children learned.

The second part of the book, written expressly for parents who would like to use our method to teach their children to write and read, provides step-by-step instructions on how to use the techniques of Writing to Read at home without a computer. You may not get the same results as we do with the computer. We don't know if the impact of the computer outweighs the impact of the parent on the child, but be prepared for a little less. We hope that IBM will eventually make the system available to parents, but meanwhile we'll tell you how you can adapt and modify these classroom activities and how to use the electric typewriter as a valuable adjunct to learning to write and read. These chapters explain how to improvise your own teaching materials, which children's books to use for early reading experiences, and how to get your child started in the right direction on the road to writing and reading, how much time to spend in learning activities, and how to judge progress.

If your child is already in the program in school (and more than 100,000 children are), we'll describe some activities for you and your child to do at home that complement those being used in the school.

Some of what you'll find in this book may seem strange to you because it doesn't conform to the way you were taught to read. You may even question the efficacy of some of our methods. But don't be concerned, because every facet of the Writing to Read System has been thoroughly tested, successfully used, and has received validation from the Educational Testing Service in Princeton, New Jersey, which, after a two-year evaluation, stated that "Writing to Read is an effective education program," and that it has made "a powerful impact on the writing and reading skills of the children."

Writing to Read, unlike most teaching programs, is a system of instruction rather than a single activity. For you to be able to use this system with your children at home it's necessary that you understand the system's various components, why they are included and when they are included, and that you gain an overall feeling for the way these components are organized. The following overview of Writing to Read, which will be elaborated throughout the book, will help you conceptualize the ideas behind the system and the way in which it works.

## WRITING TO READ IN BRIEF

Writing to Read is a computer-based instructional system designed to develop the writing and reading skills of kindergarten and first grade children. In the schools, the system works within the context of a planned learning center, a room in which students use a variety of equipment and language arts materials organized at four basic learning stations. The children use a computer, a set of instructional and game diskettes, an electric typewriter, a cassette tape player, and various sensory materials in different portions of the program.

In the program students learn to:

- Use the alphabetic principle which lets them write anything they can say
- Use a consistent phonemic spelling system
- Use the computer, which acts as a guide and tutor
- Discover the joy of language
- Develop their ability to express their ideas and manipulate the English language
- Use a typewriter.

The history of Writing to Read dates back to the early 1970s, when I began to assemble my studies of the research on how children take the first steps that lead to learning to read and write. At that time, computer technology was advancing quickly, and it was just beginning to seem feasible and practical to create an economical computer-based learning system that would effectively teach real skills, actually teach subject matter.

Knowing that reading is a key element in all learning and that the teaching of reading and writing was, and is, the most controversial of all academic subjects, I set out to construct a learning system that would produce effective results, quickly if possible, and satisfy the instructional needs of students, teachers, and parents all at the same time. The early testing of Writing to Read was conducted in an elementary school in Stuart, Florida, a small community about ninety miles north of Miami. The student population in the experimental group was mixed both racially and economically.

Writing to Read is designed for one purpose: to improve the learning of writing and reading in kindergarten and first grade children and to reduce the presently high levels of failure. But to teach children to read and write, and to make it not only intelligible but fun, is no easy task. To accomplish our ends we have combined current and past educational thought on the relationship of the two distinct skills involved in writing and reading. We used the work of Piaget, Pavlov, Skinner, Montessori, Orton, and others, as well as our own work, to provide the theoretical foundations for our effort. The key element of their studies and ours, structuring the thinking processes of the child, was then adapted to the sophisticated, multiple technology of the interactive computer with voice capability.

In creating Writing to Read four main ideas were braided to produce a complete learning system:

1.  *The alphabetic principle—phonemic spelling:*
    Since roughly 50 percent of the words of English are phonemically irregular, a complex system of rules has been created to make the process of encoding and decoding easier. It was

clear from the outset that it would be necessary for us to eliminate temporarily the contradiction of trying to teach the encoding of a language that is only half encodable. The single most common word in English is *the,* yet it's pronounced "thu." When the most common word in a language is considered an exception for spelling, there is clearly a problem of major proportions. Our simplified phonemic system overcomes this barrier.

2. *Multi-sensory activities:* All the senses—sight, touch, hearing, taste, and smell—are entry points for sending data to the brain (even the tongue can be used to sense the shape and texture of an object), and things are learned better if more than one sense is engaged during the learning process. Research confirms that a multi-sensory approach will improve learning. With this in mind, the development and the arrangement of the activities and materials in Writing to Read involve as many of the senses as possible. It's also true that children vary greatly in the dominance of their separate senses. One child may look at something intently, while another has a more acute sense of feel, and yet another hears more sharply. Interestingly, these points of focus in a single child may change from task to task depending on what is being learned. For this reason the materials in Writing to Read vary in their sensory appeal and give the child a full menu of choices.

3. *Complete exploitation of the characteristics of the computer with voice capability:* The computer, as an educational tool, has thus far been overpraised and underused. The Writing to Read computer program combines the lessons of the past with the concepts of the future in producing a series of diskettes that have turned com-

plex programming techniques into a learning system that is simple enough to be self-managed by a child just starting school.

4. *The use of logic and reason in learning:* For children who are learning to write and read, turning their thoughts into words, making their speech visible, is a logic-rooted task, and the three elements above reach those logic roots. Children need to recognize that letters are symbols for the sounds in the words they utter. Learning those symbol-sounds makes it possible to write—that is, to encode all the words they can speak (and children quickly understand that they are able to "talk with their fingers on paper"). The system allows the normal child to write at the upper levels of his ability to think and talk, and to perform this complicated task in the matter of only a few months, which is more quickly than we had believed possible.

# CHAPTER 2

# THE ALPHABETIC PRINCIPLE AND PHONEMIC SPELLING: KEYS TO WRITING AND READING

The Queen and King

Oncs there livd a queen and king. Thay livd in a kasow. One day they were feeding there babes. There was a witch that wanit to kast a spell on the queen. the queen was trying to get some fresh air. She saw the witch. The witch saw her. She put her head out the window. She told the king to do something. He got a steck to hit her on the head. The king was comin up to the window when the witch put her head in. the king hit her on her head. Then the witch was gone and the queen and the babes and the king thay livd safle and happily ever after.

The Writing to Read System is a unique and exciting experience for Wake County (Raleigh, NC) kindergarten students. Students develop a very special skill—the ability to write *all* that they can say. They bring this skill with them to first grade so that the possibilities of what can be taught have been greatly expanded.

Joyce D. Zeh,
Language Arts Coordinator

THE COMPLETE Writing to Read System was assembled like
the pieces of a puzzle as we determined what kinds of learning techniques worked best with a broad range of children.
Each time a piece of the puzzle fit, we put it in place. Our
theory was then subjected to rigorous field testing to find
out if we had been successful in transferring our abstract
ideas into practical, precisely engineered exercises that produce lasting results.

The educational theory behind Writing to Read is ec-
lectic; that is, we borrowed from a number of streams of
thought on the subjects of early learning, the development
of language and writing skills, and computer science. I'll
explain these theories in detail in due course, but I think
it will be helpful if we immediately define and explain two
of the terms which are keys to Writing to Read:

- *The Alphabetic Principle:* This giant invention
  of the human mind gave us a letter symbol for
  each sound we speak. Learning the skill of combining the twenty-six letters of the alphabet to
  form words is called writing.
- *Phonemic Spelling:* The phonemic system of
  spelling (the more familiar term is *phonics*)
  avoids the inconsistencies of English spelling as
  well as the premature emphasis on correct
  spelling in children's early writing. We have established forty-two* phonemes, which are letter-
  sound combinations, and these help children realize that speech sounds can be directly written
  or typed and that, therefore, with practice, they
  can write any word they can say. These phonemes give children the ability to use the basic
  pronunciation key of dictionaries for the rest of
  their lives.

Children in the Writing to Read program learn these
two principles concurrently, and while this learning is tak-

---

*I am indebted to Godfrey Dewey, whose World English Spelling (WES) Alphabet,
modified, is the basis of the Writing to Read System's phonemic alphabet.

ing place they begin to develop the ability to express their ideas and manipulate the English language both verbally and on paper. One of the enormous side effects of this learning is that they almost immediately discover the joy and nuance of language itself.

We feel that an understanding of the alphabetic principle is fundamental to the process of learning to write and read. Our English alphabet and all other alphabets are an accumulation of symbols, each of which at one time represented a distinctive sound made in that language. But in English we have forty-two sounds and twenty-six letters. The basic function of the alphabet is to represent a sound with a symbol. Once that trick has been learned, it's possible to construct any word that comes out of your mouth. So when someone says "mouth," it's necessary to know only that *m* is the "mmm" sound, that "ow" may be written *ou,* and that "thhh" is the digraph *th.* The next step is to understand that each of these symbol-sounds can be used over and over again to make new words. This is the alphabetic principle at its briefest. To understand better its magic, let's take a closer look.

Until the invention of an alphabet, a word was a mark, a sign, or a picture, as in the Egyptian hieroglyph, or an abbreviated picture, an abstract symbol, as in Chinese calligraphy. Those symbols represented a single word. With that type of graphic there was a need for a symbol for every single thing in the language of that civilization. In Chinese this meant, and still means, more than 30,000 characters.

The alphabetic principle was the stroke of genius that put on a piece of clay a symbol that represented a discreet sound made in the spoken language of a particular civilization. It turns out that all the languages of the world can be represented by some twenty to sixty characters, not all of which are written in Roman letters. English uses approximately forty sounds to speak itself, and our alphabet is derived from the Roman. Some of the alphabet letters representing those forty sounds are used in combinations called digraphs (*th* or *sh* or *ch*) or, if they are vowels, diphthongs (*au* and *aw* and *oo*). This symbol system, this alphabet, makes it possible to represent the more than 500,000 words that constitute English.

The Sumerians developed the prototype of the alphabet we use some 3,100 years B.C. They pressed their invention in clay with sticks to make wedge-shaped, cuneiform characters. The forms and shapes made by the stick constituted the graphic symbols for the sounds of Sumerian speech. The entire world's alphabetic writing is derivative of this discovery. The Greeks have been given credit for inventing the first true alphabet because theirs contained the first letter forms for vowel sounds.

It is important to note that the original alphabet had no vowels because people had great difficulty visualizing the vowel sounds, which are harder to hear than consonants. Children to this day share this difficulty. If a person says "hear," you can hear the "h" and the "r," and if only *hr* is written and put in context, it can be readily understood. The fact that *hr* accomplishes the work of four letters obscured, for centuries, the very existence of the vowel sounds. It's not surprising then that teachers know that children have much more difficulty learning vowels than consonants.

Of course, the original alphabet went through more evolutionary changes both great and small before Noah Webster wrote the first American dictionary in the late 1700s and codified the conventions of spelling. He was preceded by Dr. Samuel Johnson in England, who similarly froze English spelling. Before that time, correct spelling, or the lack of it, was not considered a problem of intellect or competence, only a lack of standardization. And in the final analysis, Webster didn't really make many changes in our rather contradictory way of trying to spell words. He simply dropped the letter *u* from *colour* and *humour* and reversed the final *re* in *theatre,* although Benjamin Franklin had urged him to go much further in clarifying our spelling. It was left to others to make that effort, and the fact is that a system of simplified spelling has never been accepted, though playwright Bernard Shaw, President Theodore Roosevelt (his attempt to simplify spelling through the publications of the government printing office lasted one month), Colonel McCormick and his *Chicago Tribune,* and even religious leader Brigham Young all made efforts to change the system and end its irregularities. As proof of their frustrations, there isn't a single sound in English today that can't be represented graphically in more than one way to produce the same sound.

One example will place the problem in perspective. Not long ago, I was lecturing on this point to an audience of college teachers, and in the question and answer session following my remarks a reading specialist asked if I didn't feel I was exaggerating the irregularity of spelling by using *sugar* as an example of *s* being used for "sh" when that was practically the only word, if not the only word, in English that used that spelling for that purpose. My answer was, "Are you sure?" In fact there are more than a dozen ways of spelling "sh" including *ti* in *motion,* the *oc* in *ocean,* and *se* in *nauseous.* And why *ti, oc,* and *se* should all be pronounced "sh" is a mystery to all but the most arcane students.

Therefore, writing phonemically can be presented to the child as a logical process that temporarily circumvents the need to understand the irregularities of spelling. A child can say to himself, "I can hear sounds coming from my mouth and I need to learn to write the symbols for those sounds so that I can see them." We call it talking with your fingers on paper.

Early examples look like this:

Did you ever sē a fās in a vās
Did you ever sē a snāk in a cāk

The frend cām over to my hous to spend the nīt

I like bacon. Bacon is hot and it is good. It is stīkē.
It is delishus.

We postpone the problem of learning to read with an irregular alphabetic system by learning to write as the first step in understanding what reading is all about. That is, words are speech made visible on paper. Making writing the central task fits the requirements of child-reasonableness. Children can understand what they are doing in taking the sounds that come from their mouths in strings called words, hearing those sounds, and learning a graphic symbol for those sounds. Everything that comes out of the child's mouth can be physically represented on paper. This is the alphabetic principle in practice.

The alphabetic principle the children learn is exactly the same principle adults use automatically every day, the act of combining letters in various ways to write and speak the words of English. In Writing to Read the computer program serves as a guide and tutor to systematically help children learn to apply this principle when speaking and writing words, sentences, and stories.

The alphabetic principle is not a difficult concept to grasp. The use of phonemic spelling and the creation of a phonemic alphabet require a more thorough explanation.

We hadn't gone far into our research before we discovered that the complex rules and exceptions to the standard spelling system are as confusing to youngsters today as they were to us when we were learning to spell. Of course, we can find the reasons for this confusion if we look at the extraordinarily rich evolution of English, an evolution that has placed a number of obstacles in the path of logical alphabetic spelling.

Derived from the Celtic, Latin, Germanic Anglo-Saxon, French, Middle English, Shakespearean English, Anglo-English, and American English, our language now has a huge number of sharp differences between the way we pronounce and the way we spell words. Many words we use today have a final e because in the Anglo-Saxon every letter in every word was pronounced. For example, the word *have* was pronounced "haveh," and the e had a function. We still spell *have* the same way, but the e has lost its purpose. The month of April was once *Aprille,* and it was pronounced "A-pril-le."

There are many such examples and they make writing alphabetically in English a hazardous and arbitrary task in which even good spellers often get caught perpetrating mayhem on words like *accommodate, necessary, separate, grammar,* and many more.

Some other common examples will further illustrate why this problem is so difficult to overcome. Many sounds have variations in spelling, and many spellings can be pronounced in different ways:

- We can say "eir" as in *their* and *there* and *they're*.
- The words *hair, bear,* and *bare* illustrate three spellings for the same sound, but "ear" in *hear* and "are" in the word *are* inexplicably change into new sounds.
- The common sound "oo" is the same in *do, due, through, threw, to, too,* and *two.* These spellings, however, change sounds in *go* and *so* and *rough* and *women.*
- The sound "sh" is spelled in many ways, including its use in *shove, sugar, ocean, motion,* and *nauseous.*

Only some linguists who have studied the history of word changes can logically understand these differences. As teachers and parents we unfortunately tend to overlook the confusion these irregularities bring to children in the beginning stages of learning to write and read.

If the rules of spelling are so difficult, how then do we go about teaching them to children? First, we need to recognize that there are too many rules and too many exceptions for young children to learn and apply. It's just too complex for little children. Therefore, we have constructed an alphabet that is mostly consistent without resorting to special effects such as color codes and new letters. The research we did in Writing to Read shows that the temporary use of our phonemic alphabet causes children to notice, if not understand, the arbitrary nature of standard spelling, and they soon see that they must learn nonalphabetic spelling to write many common words. Happily, this seems to replace the sense of guilt over spelling difficulties in the tender psyches of the children with a recognition that words can sometimes be both illogical and humorous.

Therefore, giving children such rules as "When two vowels go walking, the first vowel does the talking" really teaches them generalizations whose exceptions only cause confusion. This rule ignores the frequency with which *ei* and *ie,* as in *eight* and *height,* contradict this rule. But *ei* in *eight* does obey the spelling jingle "Use *i* before *e* except after *c* or when it sounds like *a,* as in *neighbor* or *weigh.* Then again, *hear* obeys the first-vowel rule, but *bear, cough, touch,* and *you* violate the rule, and *mountain* violates it twice.

We also found that the insistence on standard, correct spelling that follows rules like those above inhibits the ability of many children to write at all, and it has the secondary effect of squelching a child's natural desire to write. When children are corrected early and often in their first attempts to spell, they quickly feel hurt and discouraged. It focuses their minds on the wrong goal in the wrong order of priority. Have something to write first, then learn to edit later.

To overcome this problem, we developed a relatively consistent, uncluttered phonemic spelling system. I say relatively consistent because it deliberately isn't perfect. The forty-two letter-sound combinations we use help children realize that the sounds of their speech can be directly written (encoded). Their eyes shine when they "see" that this idea makes it possible to write anything they can say.

The alphabetic principle of writing words the way they sound and a phonemic spelling system that postpones the need to spell perfectly before writing a word are twin ingredients in the Writing to Read System, and they work together with the computer and the other physical components to form a complete learning system.

Because learning how to write phonemically is such an important element in the Writing to Read method of teaching, I want to go into the subject in more detail for those who were not taught by the phonics method and for those who may have learned to read phonetically but who have forgotten most, if not all, of what they once learned.

Teachers, administrators, and parents always ask two questions whenever I'm explaining the use of phonemes. The first is "Why do you use such an alphabet?" and the second is "Won't children have to unlearn what you have taught them so they will be able to spell correctly for the rest of their lives?"

The answer to the first question is that we use a phonemic system because the research over the last forty years has shown that the use of phonics is a more effective way to teach children how to learn to read than the whole word or "look-say" method of recognition. Phonemes are easy to comprehend, and we have found that learning happens sooner and better when a child can make sense of what he or she is doing.

We use the phonemes on page 16.

To the second question, we are able to say from experience that the process of learning to spell correctly, usually occurs in short order, and more importantly, it occurs naturally, without trauma. Later, we'll explain how we encourage children to note correct spelling as they listen to and look at the words in children's classic and modern storybooks.

Piaget and Bruner independently stressed the importance of making the learning act and the materials to foster that learning logical to a child. We saw, therefore, the need to examine what the act of reading was in all its parts. From this analysis of a very complex act and our research observations of hundreds of children we reached the conclusion that the act of writing, of making speech visible, could be made into a series of steps that children could understand, and that the ability to read would follow quickly.

What, then, is the logical progression in learning to write? If we look to historical development, we find remarkable parallels between the milestones in humanity's ability to write words and the natural stages in a child's progress in learning that same skill. First comes speech. Talking is a miracle of the human child and comes to babies generally in the first year of life. Scribbling and attempts to draw pictures, to make marks that tell stories, characterize children by their third and fourth years of life. At that stage a few children will write an occasional word remembered from a cereal box or from watching television. The impulse to write is strong.

This is perhaps a good place to point out why we teach writing before reading, a question often asked by educators as well as parents. The answer is that in historical development writing came before reading. Unlike the question of whether the chicken or the egg came first, we know writ-

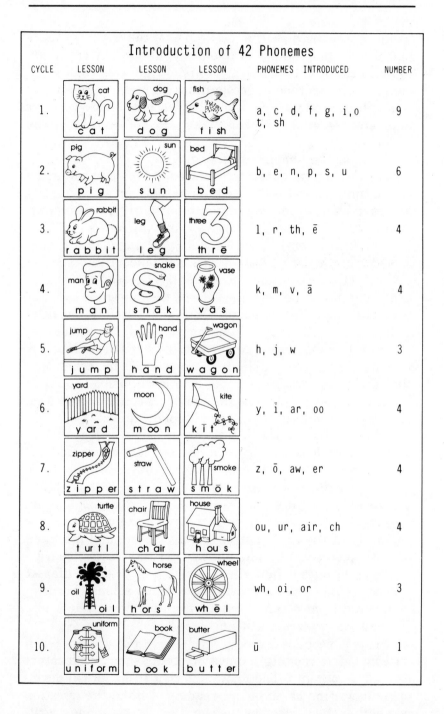

## Introduction of 42 Phonemes

| CYCLE | LESSON | LESSON | LESSON | PHONEMES INTRODUCED | NUMBER |
|---|---|---|---|---|---|
| 1. | cat — c a t | dog — d o g | fish — f i sh | a, c, d, f, g, i, o t, sh | 9 |
| 2. | pig — p i g | sun — s u n | bed — b e d | b, e, n, p, s, u | 6 |
| 3. | rabbit — r a b b i t | leg — l e g | three — th r ē | l, r, th, ē | 4 |
| 4. | man — m a n | snake — s n ā k | vase — v ā s | k, m, v, ā | 4 |
| 5. | jump — j u m p | hand — h a n d | wagon — w a g o n | h, j, w | 3 |
| 6. | yard — y ar d | moon — m oo n | kite — k ī t | y, ī, ar, oo | 4 |
| 7. | zipper — z i p p er | straw — s t r a w | smoke — s m ō k | z, ō, aw, er | 4 |
| 8. | turtle — t ur t l | chair — ch air | house — h ou s | ou, ur, air, ch | 4 |
| 9. | oil — oi l | horse — h or s | wheel — wh ē l | wh, oi, or | 3 |
| 10. | uniform — u n i f or m | book — b oo k | butter — b u t t er | ū | 1 |

ing preceded reading in human history. We know this because there had to be a writer before there was a reader, and because the urge to write, to decorate, to convey a message, prevails throughout history. Archaeologists and anthropologists have yet to discover a primitive society that doesn't show evidence of this basic urge to communicate through some form of visible-symbol system. This natural urge of early man to communicate and to ornament his cave walls with paintings is a preliminary development to writing.

I have a feeling about the conversation that occurred as a curious observer looked over the shoulder of the very first cave painter. "Tell me," the person asked, "what does it say?" The query seems to be likely because picture drawing, the representational art of its time, was an effort to tell a story about hunters, animals, their gods, and other events that affected the life of the painter and the group with which he lived.

As the world became more populous there was a need for record keeping, for counting people, for surveying property lines, for keeping totals on crop production, for recording income and expenses, and for writing rules and regulations. A notation system became necessary, and the widespread invention of $x$'s (xxxxx) and the diagonal line (//////) for counting from Asia Minor to the pre-Colombian American Indian is remarkable. The cross marks and the diagonal were actually an early form of arithmetic and were often used for recording quantity. Usually a drawing of the item being counted—an animal skin, a sheaf of grain, spices—was used for identification. Thus, early symbol writing and calculating developed from the needs of merchants involved in commerce. And we can be sure that kings and tax collectors made such notation systems a governmental function as well.

The development of writing proceeded from accurate picture drawing to the ideogram, a shorthand abstraction—of a bird or a house, for example—that was a fast substitute for more complete representations. The important point, so easily forgotten, is that until someone had the impulse or the need to say something to someone not present, to send a message, or keep a record, there was no need to write. Historically it is clear that the first urge was to write; the second was to be understood. Reading followed writing.

There is another, nonhistorical, reason we think it's important to teach writing before reading. From the standpoint of the child, learning to write is a self-motivating task that requires action, while learning to read tends to be more passive. Children *want* to learn to read but they *love* to learn to write. This isn't hard to understand. If you can put something on paper that you want to say, it is very satisfying, very good for the ego. This is evident in the fact that when children first learn to write they begin to leave paper messages to mothers, fathers, brothers, and sisters stuck on the refrigerator door. They may be very short messages, like "I luv you" or "I luv mi dog" or "mom, I luv you," but they are attempts, and good ones, to communicate by writing.

One day one of the teachers was absent from our experimental laboratory, and two kindergarten girls she had been working with in class decided to write her a note. After some discussion between them they wrote: "Der mzzus Mrtn, we mist U." This may appear to be a primitive effort at first glance, but it is actually a sophisticated piece of writing from beginning writers who wanted to say something that was important to them and recognized that they could write a message. The observer who sees only the misspellings misses the important fact that they were using an alphabet to express phonemically the sounds that they heard when they spoke. When children make that breakthrough, they then begin to fill in the blanks where letters are missing and they begin to spell more conventionally. This is very ego satisfying; it is much more a projection of themselves than the decoding process of reading. And behind this is the importance of reason, the importance of being able to think in the process of learning. To construct that simple sentence, those children had to think. They needed to listen to the sounds coming out of their mouths in a regular order. They then needed the alphabet symbols for those sounds to write them in that same order to "make a word." That is a high act of cognition. Its validity is proved by what children at the same level of development are writing after six months in the program. The following example comes from this same class:

### The Sindrelu storree

wunts a pon a time ago thair wuz a litle gerl that livd in a house and she had a step muther is mean so mean that she locd her in the room and she had the kē in her hand. The sindrelu coon git it out uf her room. She wuz locd in her room hugrē. Wunday a leter came to the house. It sez that evrē gerl had to bē at the bol. Sindrelis step muther had her dōwing jobz so mintē jobz that she cood not git her self retē to gō to the bol. and her stepmuther and her step sisterz and her mom lefd she win into the gardin and she sat and she locd up and she saw a fairrē god muther and she sed I can not go to the bol. Yes you can. I need a pukin and she went and got a pukin and she sed she needid sum mīs to trn into horses and she trnd a old mouse into a cōch man and off tha went to the bol and the fairreē god muther sed that the spel will be brōcin bī minīt and time wuz fling. Bog Bog went the bel and sindurelu ran dan the palis sterz and wun glas sliper fel and sindrelu ran to the house and the prints sed that hooz ever foot fits in this liper i will marē her and thā trīd evere gerlz foot and sindrelu and the prints livd haule ever afder.

This example brings up another point that deserves mention. We do correct phonemically misspelled words. This is not necessarily aimed at achieving standard spelling but at achieving phonemic clarity. So, if a sentence reads, "I shet the dor," the child needs help in hearing the vowel sound "u" in the word *shut* but need not be corrected for spelling *door* as *dor,* which is phonemically correct. In other words, it isn't necessary to try to accomplish the entire task of phonemic and absolutely correct spelling at one time. Working toward phonemic clarity is more productive for early writing, and there is plenty of time to move on to more accurate spelling.

Our theory is that children will have to face the world of conventional spelling and its phonemic eccentricity soon enough. If we can delay that encounter with orthographic ambiguities by making them competent users of the alphabetic principle, we know they will learn to enjoy the written word.

# CHAPTER 3

# WRITING TO READ IN DETAIL

### A Message From Planet Zorron

I came from the planet Zorron. Everyday the temperchure is fourty degrees below zerox. I wear 1000 jackets . . . the planet Zorron is 1000 times bigger than our sun. Zorron is the only planet in the Alpharo solar stem. There are 9 suns. 8 of them are black holes and the last one is a white dwarf that has sun spots. When UFO'S come by they all said gosh are you ugly! What is this entellegent life? And all of them made there ship go up and down.

Jimmy, Kindergarten

When the Slīder children come to my house to play all four of us have a club. We bring money but we haven't had the club four days. Scott and Sara come on Thursdays. Scott and Sandi are the presedents and the vice presedents. Me and Sara have to be dumb lookouts and nobody every comes.

I'm me! I'm special! I like being me because I'm the oldest child in the family. I'm only seven years old. I have blue eyes. I have a little sister. My birthday is in January 15. I like school. I go to Smith Elamenty School. I have a mother and father. My mothers says I'm inportint to her. But I don't like my name witch is Sarakeck. I wish it was Angela. I like to eat tacos and Pizza. My hobby is to color. I have four pets they are rabbit, turtle, toad and frog. When I growup I want to be a techer. I wish I could be rich or butiful.

WHEN ASKED TO explain the Writing to Read System in a
sentence, I respond that Writing to Read is a computer-
based instructional system designed to develop the writing
and reading skills of kindergarten and first grade children.
This is an easy and precise, yet incomplete, explanation
because Writing to Read is much more than a computer
program that makes use of old techniques in a new format.
Writing to Read combines the teaching of the alphabetic
principle, the use of a phonemic alphabet, the newly discovered power of the computer, the proven value of the electric typewriter, and the use of a variety of sensory-learning
materials to create a complete learning system that is comprehensive and relies upon children's capacity to think and
reason while they learn.

In the Writing to Read classroom, kindergarten and
first grade children use this variety of equipment and lan-
guage-arts materials at six learning stations which focus
on one or more of the elements that form the Writing to
Read System. These stations are called:

- The Computer Station
- The Writing/Typing Station
- The Work Journal Station
- The Listening Library Station
- The Multi-Sensory Materials Station
- The Make Words Station

The equipment and materials used at these stations
include an IBM PCjr Personal Computer and instructional
diskettes, an IBM Selectric typewriter, cassette tape players, prerecorded audio cassettes, audio headphones, classic
children's books, Work Journals, clay, felt-tip pens, chalk
and slate, ultrasoft lead pencils and paper, and sand trays
lined with black emery cloth.

Thus, the high technology of the computer has been
augmented by other learning activities that are not based
in the world of high technology at all. We use typewriting
because definitive research done more than fifty years ago
has shown that when children use the typewriter they learn
better. We also know that children can be encouraged to

learn writing and reading skills by listening to someone read them stories, by making letters and words out of clay, by using chalk and slate to write letters and words, by tracing letters with their fingers in a tray of sand, and by writing on unlined paper with a soft lead pencil.

Except for the use of the interactive computer there is really nothing strikingly new here. These are all practices and materials that have been used with variations, formally and informally, by parents and teachers for generations. It's the combination of these activities with the technology of the computer, and the application of the learning theory behind Writing to Read that makes our program uniquely effective.

The Writing to Read System is based on my more than thirty-five years as an educator, first as a teacher in a one-room schoolhouse, then as a principal, and finally as a superintendent and consultant to various government education agencies. I brought this experience with me when I began working on the Writing to Read concept. Now, after seven years of intensive research, design, refinement, and field testing of the program it is in operation in hundreds of schools in this country and abroad.

In this time, I have observed thousands of children in groups and individually and mined the research of the leading learning theorists and child development specialists. Some of this research was done in our classroom laboratory and some while sitting on school playgrounds with a tape recorder documenting on tape the words children use with each other. I used these tapes to compile a word list of children's most common oral vocabulary. Combining my word-frequency list with those tabulated by others, I had the basic vocabulary for a writing and reading program.

All of this has led me to some basic conclusions about early learning, conclusions that indicate most normal children:

- Come to school able to speak more than 2,000 words, and they can use that vocabulary in a sophisticated syntax nearly as complex as that

used by adults. They can and do speak in compound and complex sentences which they connect with *and, but, because,* and *so*
- Can quickly use these language skills as they
  learn to write the sounds of English in words,
  sentences, and stories
- Learn better if the material is organized to encourage them to think and to find a logical order
  in the material to be learned
- Can learn to apply the alphabetic principle of
  phonemic spelling to write and read their own
  words, sentences, and stories in a shorter time
  than we had believed necessary
- Make the transition from phonemic to standard
  spelling easily and naturally
- Learn better when several of the senses are involved at the same time
- Learn better in a structured environment that
  is risk-free and where they manage their own
  progress and learning activities
- Learn better if they produce their own hard copy
  as evidence of learning
- Should regularly share their work with their
  peers and their parents and are anxious to do
  so
- Have greater success with a program whose diversity fits the many ways they learn, as opposed to one which tries to fit all children into
  only one learning method
- Learn in pairs better than alone
- Retain their skills and continue their progress
  into the upper grades of their school.

Writing to Read was developed with all of these facts
in mind, and it has demonstrated what it can do by passing
the ultimate test of rigorous field evaluation. The results
have persuaded a growing number of people in the education community that there is an alternative, a better alternative, to standard reading programs.

I previously pointed out the results of the evaluation of Writing to Read by the Educational Testing Service. The specifics of that evaluation led ETS to these major conclusions:

1. *The Writing to Read approach works:* It functions well as a complex set of interconnecting parts; children can handle the technology and the movement from work station to work station.

2. *Children learn with Writing to Read:* On standardized reading tests, kindergarten and first grade Writing to Read students, on the average, progressed faster than the national norm; kindergarten students increased their scores an average of 15 percentile points.

3. *Children in Writing to Read write better than comparison groups:* On rating scales developed by ETS, students in the program rated higher.

4. *Students in the program read better:* In reading, kindergarten Writing to Read students had a significant advantage over comparison students.

5. *Students in the program spell better:* Writing to Read participants performed slightly better than other students in spelling.

6. *Teachers like Writing to Read:* Teachers' observations indicate that students in the program write and read better than other students and spend more time writing.

7. *Parents like Writing to Read:* Ninety-three percent of parents want their school to continue to use the program; they report greater progress in reading and that their children like the program.

Such results, as convincing as they may be, are more useful in the world of formal education than with parents who are anxious about the ability of their young children to learn to read and write in the classrooms of the 1980s.

For this reason, I'm going to explain in detail, and in

terms more suited to concerned parents, what Writing to Read is and how parents can use its principles whether or not they have a computer.

The first thing we want children to understand is that they can write what they say—that is, they can write all the words they speak so casually every day—and the program provides a set of activities designed for this purpose. We encourage children to write. If a child can say *train* the child can write *train*. If a child can say *steam shovel* the child can write *steam shovel* in a form that is easily recognizable even though it may not be spelled correctly. This is true for any other word no matter how complex, including "feroshus," "refrigrater," and "graguating," all words written by five-year-olds in our program. It's obvious that although they are not spelled in the standard manner, they are readable.

In Writing to Read children learn to hear the sounds in their words, and they learn to write the alphabet symbols for those sounds. We have invented no new letters or letter combinations. The forty-two common English phonemes are introduced by using thirty words to illustrate them. Each word is the object of a series of lessons on the computer and additionally in a set of workbooks we call Work Journals.

In the program used in the schools, children work daily at the computer and at the other learning stations, whose activities reinforce and extend the computer-based lessons.

## THE WRITING TO READ WORK STATIONS

*The Computer Station:* At this station the children follow the instructions on the program diskettes which guide them through one of the three words in each of the ten cycles of the system. Each day they spend twelve to fifteen minutes at the computer listening to words and sounds, then saying the words and sounds, typing letters to make words, and responding with rhythmic chanting, hand clapping and foot stamping to the vocal and visual commands of the computer.

*The Writing/Typing Station:* Children type words derived from that day's work on the computer or from previous

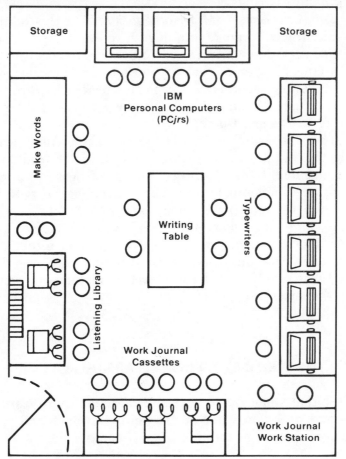

Storage

Storage

Make Words

IBM
Personal Computers
(PCjrs)

Typewriters

Writing
Table

Listening Library

Work Journal
Cassettes

Work Journal
Work Station

lessons, and as their skills progress, they begin to write and type their own words, sentences, and stories.

*The Work Journal Station:* Here, using soft lead pencils, the children write the letters and words covered in the computer session. They also fill in boxes in a chart on the back cover, where they document their progress. This helps them determine for themselves when they are ready to move on to the next step or the next cycle.

*The Listening Library Station:* At this table, children put on earphones and listen to tape-recorded readings of children's classics such as *Mike Mulligan's Steam Shovel, Peter Rabbit, The Three Bears,* and *Carrot Seed* while they learn to follow the stories with their fingers in the book after many hearings.

*The Multi-Sensory Materials Station:* Here the children are encouraged to make letters with rolled strings of clay, trace a letter shape in a tray of sand or rice lined with fine, black emery paper (at home you can line the tray with gelatin powder—a sweet finger is an effective reward), use soft lead pencils and unlined paper or chalk and slate for writing letters and words.

*The Make Words Station:* Children take turns showing each other duplicate drawings of the objects on the computer programs and, later, pictures of airplanes, horses, flowers, and other common objects. Each picture has the word for the object written on the back. The word can only be seen by the child who is doing the presenting. The partner uses letters on cards about two inches square to form the word much as in Scrabble. The children tutor each other as they take turns identifying the picture and making the words with the letters.

## THE WRITING TO READ LEARNING CYCLE

So that you can better visualize each of these stations let's look at the way one of the words in the second cycle lesson is covered in detail. The word is *pig.*

At the Computer

After the two disks are inserted in the computer, the child, sitting with a partner, sees a selection menu on the screen that looks like this:

```
        -------------------------------------------
CYCLE  1   SELECTION MENU
        -------------------------------------------


        1.     Pig

        2.     Sun

        3.     Bed

        4.     Mastery Test

        5.     Make Words
```

After the child has typed the number, *1* in this case, a graphic picture of an orange pig appears along with the word *pig* in green.

Now the very pleasant, nondemanding voice begins the lesson:

This is a pig.
[The picture is removed. The word *pig* remains.]
See the word pig.
Say pig.
Say pig.
[The word *pig* flashes as if in response to the child's
    voice. The word moves, a letter at a time, from
    the center of the screen to each letter's alpha-
    betical position around the edge of the screen.]
This is the sound p, p.
Say p, type p. [When the *p* is typed, the letter moves
    from its place on the periphery of the screen to
    the center of the screen.]

Say pig.
This is the sound i [short sound], i, say i.
Type i.
Say pig.
This is the sound g, g, say g.
Type g.
Say pig. Say pig.
Type pig. Say pig. Type pig.

The screen then shows the phonemes that have been covered so far in the cycle and in previous cycles, and the letters *p, i,* and *g* move from the center of the screen to their places on the outside edges. The voice picks up again:

Say p, say pig. Type p.
Say i, say pig. Type i.
Say g, say pig. Type g.
Say pig. Type pig. Type pig. Yes. [If an incorrect
    key is pressed at this point or at any point, the
    voice repeats the command to type the letter that
    is wanted. No error is recorded, nor does an in-
    correct letter ever appear on the screen.]

The letters now move quickly to the center of the screen and then move back to the periphery. The voice then says:

Say p, say p-pp-p-p. [This is done in a rhythm that
    is one long, two short, and two long "p" sounds.]
Say i-ii-i-i [in rhythm].
Say g, say g-gg-g-g [in rhythm].
Say pig. Type pig. Say pig. Type pig.
Say p, say p-pp-p-p and clap your hands.
Say i, say i-ii-i-i and clap your hands.
Say g, say g-gg-g-g and clap your hands. [The qual-
    ity of the voice is always encouraging and never
    judgmental.]

The next cycle of commands continues:

> Say pig. Type pig.
> Say pig. Type pig.
> Say p, say p-pp-p-p and stamp your foot.
> Say i, say i-ii-i-i and stamp your foot.
> Say g, say g-gg-g-g and stamp your foot.
> Say pig. Type pig. Say pig. Type pig.
> Say pig. Say pig. Type pig. Say pig. Type pig.
> Say pig. Type pig.
> End of pig. All done.

When all of these actions have been completed, the machine gives five beeps that signify the end of the cycle word. At that point the selection menu reappears and offers the same choices for the next session. Children generally complete a cycle word such as *pig* in ten to twelve minutes. They are not permitted to remain at the computer longer than fifteen minutes. When the child has completed all three words in a cycle, item 4 on the menu, the Mastery Test, follows:

> Type pig. Yes [if correct].
> Type sun. Yes.
> Type bed. Yes.

If two mistakes are made on one word or too much time is taken before a response, the system automatically sends the child back to the program word in question, *bed* for example. The program repeats the picture of a bed with its word and the voice says, "This is a bed." If the child recognizes the error and immediately or later says to himself, "Oh, of course, that's how it goes," he can press a key that puts him back into the Mastery Test process, which then continues until all the words have been typed correctly.

When the Mastery Test has been successfully completed, the menu appears again and item number 5, the Make Words selection, is chosen. The computer says:

> Say ship. Say sh, type sh.
> Say sh, say ship.
> Say i. Type i. Say i. Say ship.
> Say p. Type p. Say p. Type ship.

In this part of the cycle, if a wrong key is pressed the correct letter flashes in its position on the edge of the screen until the correction is made. The several additional words in the Make Words part of the cycle are all new words made up of the letter-phonemes introduced in this cycle and previous cycles. Children are tutored into "making words" by oral and visual clues. The intent is to have them gradually begin to understand how letter-sounds, letters, can make new words.

This summarizes the complete computer session in Writing to Read, and I think if you try to put yourself in the position of a five-year-old, you can sense from your reading that the combination of responses requested is sufficient to produce, through repetition, the desired learning in most children. And of course, this is only one of the ten cycles of the program. After finishing at the computer for the day, a child can then choose to work at any of the other learning stations, all of which have activities that augment the machine-based learning.

Before explaining the activities at the other learning stations, however, I want to highlight some of the special computer features in the Writing to Read System that are different but which may not be readily apparent. I do this because these points will help you understand how the process works.

First, the program accepts correct responses at all times. It can do this even when a child hits the right key before an action is requested because it can store the response until the proper time for inserting it. Thus a very precocious child can run ahead of the computer without penalty. Just as important, the system, as we have said, does not accept, reject, or record errors. So if a child types an *o* instead of a *p,* there is no response on the screen and the original request is repeated. If the child fails to type the correct letter several times, that letter will begin to flash from its home position on the border of the screen. The correct letter is never filled in for the child by the machine nor is the child ever admonished. This is because correcting isn't learning; it is felt as a subtle form of abuse by the child.

Second, the Make Words part of the cycle enlarges a child's written vocabulary by presenting words which are new but of similar phonemic construction to those in previous lessons. It is sufficiently difficult to encourage thinking but not so difficult as to be discouraging. For example, at the completion of Cycle 1, which introduces the words *cat, dog,* and *fish,* the nine phonemes of these three words are displayed alphabetically on the edges of the screen leaving spaces for the thirty-three phonemes that are yet to be learned. The child is then asked to type the new word *fat* using three of the nine phonemes, drawn from *cat* and *fish.* If the child doesn't respond, the program tutors the child by flashing the *f* in its position on the edge of the screen and then the other letters as necessary.

Third, the accumulating phonemes in each cycle (nine in Cycle 1, six more in Cycle 2, four more in Cycle 3, and so forth) are positioned on the outer edge of the screen, and in this way a child gradually absorbs the extraordinary properties of the alphabet. A child learns, at first subliminally, then slowly more concretely and consciously, that letters operate as visible symbols of the sounds of spoken words and that the twenty-six letters in various combinations can make all the words they can speak. This is an extremely important concept to understand—that is, letters are visible representations of sound and they are reusable in other words and in different combinations. Our experience indicates that the average five-year-old captures this idea in less than two months. So rather quickly, a child begins to conceive of writing as a thinking act and this produces a sense of personal skill and self-assurance.

Fourth, the software for Writing to Read provides an intrinsic reward for children, the mastery of communication, without whistles, buzzers, and blinking lights or the excessive need for external adult approval or correction. There are no superfluous inducements, either positive or negative. Children find their joy, their internal satisfaction, in the knowledge that they have learned something completely. Of course, a parental smile is always welcome.

Fifth, we have incorporated an element in the Writing

to Read software which is not unusual in its concept but is unusual in its application. For two centuries, educators have studied the close relationship of learning, play, and laughter in children. In addition to exciting a child's early joy in knowing that he or she is learning, Writing to Read introduces, after several weeks of the program, an activity called Silly Sentences, which takes advantage of this relationship between fun and learning. Using only words drawn from the child's accumulating program vocabulary, we create unlikely juxtapositions of things and events which cause children to laugh. Sentences such as "Did you ever see a pig in a bed?" and "Did you ever see a horse in a house?" represent not only words but whole thoughts that are different enough, out of context enough, to induce children to notice, to laugh, and to learn.

Still later, games such as Cat and Mouse, and Rabbit and Turtle are introduced to guide the child toward the use of longer sentences in describing events and, at the same time, to add an element of chance and of fun. The two games revolve around the safety of the mouse in the first instance and who will win the ancient race between the tortoise and the hare in the second.

In these situations the computer does more than present information and register the child's response; it also judges the child's answers against a stored model that is sensitive to the time taken to respond (to type the whole words *mouse* or *turtle*) and the correctness of the response. Since both speed and accuracy are necessary, as the child learns to type faster, the letters move to their positions more quickly and the child progresses from typing letter by letter to typing the entire word rapidly. This practice enables us to capitalize on the computer's versatility and thus help a child progress from single-word writing to the construction of whole sentences and to increase typing speed.

The Cat and Mouse game is programmed to allow for a wide range of children's abilities. Thus the game requires its players to type the word *mouse* more quickly than the cat on the screen can catch the mouse. The speed of the game increases in proportion to the increase in the child's speed and accuracy of response. In the rabbit and turtle race the player can help the turtle by typing the needed word correctly and on time. Still, the outcome isn't always certain no matter how quickly or how accurately the player responds, because there is a random element in the program that, on occasion, tips the balance against the player no matter how fast he or she works. This uncertainty principle holds the player's interest beyond the time when attention would normally wander in a game of this kind.

We have designed these game elements into the Writing to Read System for two reasons: They aid and stimulate learning, and they enhance the appeal of the entire program for children. Our rationale has been to stress success in learning while skills are being developed and later to use these gaming elements to pit those new skills against the machine.

The incorporation of gaming strategies in the design of learning situations is based in part on the work of John Van Neumann, the mathematician whose theories were basic in the early development of computers. In the course of our own work we've found that for games of this kind to be successful as learning tools (whether computer-based or not), they must meet the following criteria (which will be valuable for parents in understanding the dynamics of playing any game with a child):

- A game must have a clearly defined goal and when that goal is reached the game is won
- Playing the game must provide the opportunity for the player to increase his or her skill in order to improve the opportunity of winning
- The skill to win every time must be elusive or very difficult, for once a game is mastered (as with Tic-Tac-Toe), it quickly loses its appeal; therefore chance elements must be introduced to make it possible for even a very skilled player to lose.

In Writing to Read we have successfully exploited the
current outer limits of the computer for teaching writing
and reading. When more advanced machines are developed,
voice activated and with greater artificial-intelligence ca-
pacities, our most sophisticated programming will again be
stretched greatly.

Now we'll examine what happens at the other learning
stations.

### The Writing/Typing Station

This is the one spot in the Writing to Read classroom
that is always filled. The qualities of the electric typewriter
seem to exert a gravitational pull on children, and they move
to it with eagerness and joy. One reason for this happy
anticipation is that the typewriter provides a perfect re-
production of the letter the child wants to write and it does
it every time. The machine helps them over a large hurdle
that stands in the path which leads to writing: the labor of
writing letters. Obviously, they must learn this skill as well,
but learning the precise formation of letters with ascenders
and descenders of exactly the right length is often confused
in schools with learning to write. Penmanship drills don't

teach writing. It's also easy to correct errors on the typewriter or make changes by backspacing and x'ing out the letters or words that need to be changed. We ask that erasers be forbidden in the Writing to Read classrooms, since writing is rewriting and children learn early to edit their own work.

Though the typewriter is conceived of as a machine for writing phrases, sentences, and whole paragraphs, it is also useful for hunting and pecking out individual words, and this is the first use children make of the technology. Before they are able to write strings of words or sentences, they use the typewriter to practice cycle words and to make occasional new words. They are far from ten-finger typists but they quickly learn the location of the letters on the keyboard. This early typing is typically in columns of words with one word on each line. Soon they begin to write short sentences characterized by the first person pronoun: "I like my dog," "I like my mother," "I like . . . ," and so on. In due time, typically in less than three months, they begin to write longer sentences and then stories like these:

### A little lost girls story

Wuns apon a time thair wus a lost child. She was scaird. Her nām wus Kelley. She had never been lost before. She had a foster familiē. She ran away. It wus dark. She did not have a flash lite. Somthing jumpd out. she wus scaird. Her mom and dad saw her asleep. Thay pickd her up. She did not wak up untill she got home. Thay gāv her waking up meduasin. but she was stel sleepey. She wus not able to talk. She wus cold so she took a warm bath. Her dady cām in the bath roem and he toll her it was okay. She never ran off agaen.

### My trip to outer space*

One day I took a trip to outer spās. On the way I saw a Marshon so I landed on Mars to see the Marshon and I made friends with him. He told me all about spās and we had lot of fun together. We wanted to land on Satern so we did and we saw a strang thing. It had a skwair head and for it's eyes it had stroberes and for it's nose it had a orng. It's body was a bunanu and it's arms were bunanus too. So me and Zaper made frends with that strang thing. We said, "What is your name?" and then he said back to us. "My name is Crist." Then we said lets play a game and I said lets play tug a war. I saw we need a rope so Zaper went back to the ship and got the rope. Ges who was the coch? Za-per. Ges who won? Me.

At all stages the children are encouraged to edit their errors and to change words by crossing out with the x key.

A word here on correcting. I know from experience that the suggestion of crossing out errors violates the standard order of things for many people. Teachers in particular seem to abhor crossovers and erasures, fingerprints, bent corners, and writing that is not on the line. Most parents have a similar problem that is born out of their own experiences

---

*Each sentence was a page in a story illustrated by the child.

in school. But there has to be a certain messiness in learning, a process of write and rewrite. These first writing attempts, available to view, to work on, to rewrite, edit, improve, and to think about, constitute a process which teaches that partial and approximate attempts are a normal part of learning without shame.

There is also a writing area at this station where children have access to paper, crayons, markers, pencils, and chalk. We encourage them to think about what they want to say and the words they want to use, to say the words and listen to the sounds inside the words. Then they can write the phonemes that represent those sounds.

I can't emphasize too strongly that penmanship is not writing. Adults tend to overemphasize calligraphy at the expense of the central purpose of writing—to say something. To write, a child first has to learn to use a writing tool, the pencil, to form the shapes that become the letters of the words, and this skill must be learned at the same time he learns the letters he is writing. Mastering the tool can sometimes be as difficult as mastering the work at hand—writing the letters and words. Cut soft lead pencils, number ones, in half. Don't use seven-inch hard lead pencils. While the struggle with the pencil continues, there is little chance of capturing a thought before it escapes. In fact, young children often forget the letters of a three-letter word while trying to master the mechanics of making a perfectly shaped letter. The nearly universal practice in schools of using paper with an inch between the lines and a dotted line halfway between the solid lines compels children to laboriously "draw" each letter as an art form, and this is another impediment that slows to a standstill the process of learning to write.

As adults we've all experienced the inability of the writing hand to keep up with the mind. The problem is compounded for a child who is just learning to form letters. This overly meticulous, often painful process requires total concentration. The tight pressing of the fingers against the bevels of the hexagonal pencil actually causes pain. The extra care needed to keep from poking the hard lead pencil point through the paper causes anxiety.

Obviously, writing "longhand" will never be obsolete
—everyone should know how to do it—but the speed of the
typewriter removes the confusion of letter formation and
the delays in thought patterns because it keeps better pace
with the flow of the mind. This conveys a feeling of power
to the writer that can't be ignored. Leap ahead with us to
what we've shown to be dramatically possible. Kindergarten
children can learn to touch-type their stories using the ten-
finger method before using the computer as a word processor. In one public school in Burlington, North Carolina,
twenty out of twenty-four kindergarten children became
"able typists" in five months.

## The Work Journal Station

This is an important stop in the Writing to Read center.
Here the children record their cycle words on paper in a
notebook called a Work Journal, and this accomplishes several things. It reinforces the computer instruction and gives
children the opportunity to write all the new phonemes of
the cycle as they appear in the new words.

The design of the Work Journals uses graphics to tell
children what to do on each page with a minimum of adult
intervention. Thus, on page one, a picture of a headset for
a tape recorder tells a child to listen to the appropriate tape
cassette with the same picture that appeared on the computer. So the word *cat* and its picture appear on the tape
cassette and on the Work Journal. The recorded voice says
the word "cat" and asks the child to put a finger under the
word. Next the voice asks the child to put his finger under
each letter and finally to write the word in a column down
the page to the bottom, where the whole word is to be written. On each of the following pages one of the sounds in the
word *cat* is illustrated with drawings of objects using that
phoneme, along with the words for the objects—for example, *cup* on one page, *apple* on another, and *tent* on a third.
Each of the words is repeated on a second line, but with the
appropriate phoneme missing. The child is asked to write
the missing letter in each case. The bottom right-hand corner of the page shows a raised hand to signal to the child
to call for a happy review or assistance.

All the journals are in the same format. They contain space for writing words from the current cycle and for creating new words. Another page, called Write Words, is blank, and there is plenty of space to practice writing words that have already been learned and for drawing pictures that illustrate any words they want to write. This is a "free" page that is open for experimentation with the newly discovered knowledge of letters and sounds.

The Progress Chart on the back cover gives us one more piece of positive reinforcement that allows each child the opportunity to mark and reward his own progress as he completes each step in the cycle.

Throughout their work at the various stations children are encouraged to pay attention to the way words are spelled in books and when possible to write "the way it is in books." Still, they are completely free to write using their own spelling and they do write "bootēful" and "ēnormus" with a great

```
┌──────────────────────────────────────────────┐
│   ┌──────────────────────────────────────┐    │
│   │   name_____  1    │    │
│   │                                      │    │
│   │  [💻]  computer     [📖] work journal │    │
│   │  ┌──────────────┬─┐ ┌──────────────┬─┐│    │
│   │  │ 1. cat       │X│ │ 1. cat       │X││    │
│   │  │ 2. dog       │X│ │ 2. dog       │ ││    │
│   │  │ 3. fish      │X│ │ 3. fish      │X││    │
│   │  │ 4. test      │X│ │ 4. test      │ ││    │
│   │  │ 5. make words│X│ │ 5. make words│ ││    │
│   │  └──────────────┴─┘ └──────────────┴─┘│    │
│   │                                      │    │
│   │  [abc] make words game  ┌──┬──┬──┐   │    │
│   │                          └──┴──┴──┘   │    │
│   │  [⌨] typewriter         ┌──┬──┬──┐   │    │
│   │                          └──┴──┴──┘   │    │
│   │  [📖🎧] listen to stories ┌──┬──┬──┐  │    │
│   │                          └──┴──┴──┘   │    │
│   │  teacher's comments:        ┌────┐    │    │
│   │                              │    │    │    │
│   │                              └────┘    │    │
│   │                                      │    │
│   │      work completed_____    │    │
│   │                    teacher signature  │    │
│   └──────────────────────────────────────┘    │
└──────────────────────────────────────────────┘
```

sense of competence. But conventional spelling soon creeps in, and it is rare to see more than a handful of children who continue to write *the* as "thu" beyond their first few attempts.

As the phonemes necessary for writing the speech sounds are learned, we have observed how a child's writing progresses through six distinct stages, and in a later chapter we'll give examples of these stages so that you will be better able to follow your own child's writing progress. The stages are:

- Writing cycle words
- Writing new words
- Writing their own phrases and sentences
- Writing sentences in logical order
- Beginning story writing
- More advanced writing characterized by narrative development and description.

The concurrent progress of children in phonemic writing and book reading continues, and as they discover they can read, they tend to transfer gradually to the spelling they see in books. It's interesting also that children show no apparent conflict between writing with phonemic spelling and the development of a sight vocabulary written with conventional spelling. When they have time to understand the spelling process, and recognize a few examples of its seeming irrationality, children taught in this manner equal or excel at conventional spelling. Thanks to the encoding system the child has learned, these words can be pronounced and understood and correct spelling soon becomes a matter of course. At this point the rewards of both writing and reading are being reaped.

This is the way the program works in the Writing to Read classroom. I realize that few homes have all the materials (and why should they?) to offer all the learning experiences suggested, but except for the computer, much of the classroom program can be duplicated by parents who are interested in their child's early learning development and in later chapters we'll explain how to do it.

## The Listening Library Station

At the Listening Station children are exposed to the culture of the book. Here they listen (with earphones) to tape recordings of stories whose tapes are correlated exactly with the printed versions of the books that they "read" while they listen. They look at the words and listen, turn the page when indicated, and take their first steps toward directly matching the spoken and the written word. In selecting these books we've carefully chosen modern and classic stories that have proven appeal to children. Quality children's books are magnetically appealing, and listening to good stories makes young people want to read on their own.

At this station, children begin to realize, as they follow the print of the story, that the letters they use to write their own speech sounds are the same ones they see in the books they are reading. They will, after listening to their favorite

stories over and over, begin to follow the words exactly with their fingers. Soon they will talk softly to themselves along with the recorded voice. Both the finger pointing and the talking are highly desirable and should be encouraged and greeted with joy.

The Multi-Sensory Materials Station

In this area children find soft, dark-colored clay to roll into strings that are then shaped into letters, a sand tray with a thin coating of sand covering fine, black emery cloth in which they trace letters with their fingers, chalk and slate, magnetic letters, and felt letters. They use these materials to reinforce, with touch, the idea of letters and to form their names and their first words.

## The Make Words Station

The purpose of this station is to help children learn the alphabetic principle—that is, letters stand for the sounds in their speech. The materials at this table may include letter cards, wooden block letters, letter stamps, magnetic letters, and any other form of individual letter that is appropriate. These letters can be used for naming pictures, playing word games, or word bingo.

These few pages summarize the entire Writing to Read System. We have tried to include enough detail to make it understandable and useful to parents. We didn't want to bombard you with minutiae; yet we did want to make it clear that the system is strongly based in educational theory and that it is designed to develop writing and reading skills quickly. The next chapter puts our enthusiasm in greater perspective.

# CHAPTER 4

# WHAT WRITING TO READ IS NOT

It has been exciting to observe small children become actively involved, without inhibitions, in writing and then reading their own thoughts to others. This program encourages each child to progress at his or her own rate. Some make words; others write sentences; and still others are stimulated to be authors of their own little books as they write, edit, type and then illustrate their stories. Enthusiasm is evident in inter-disciplinary activities, as kindergartners record science experiences, compose "word" math problems, and write letters to friends.

Rosalind Bowling,
Kindergarten teacher,
Raleigh, North Carolina

The Writing to Read System has made a tremendous difference in the amount and quality of the writing and reading students can do in kindergarten and first grade. Impoverished students especially have shown a remarkable response to this early instruction.

Dr. Mary Jane McReynolds,
Principal, Briarcliff Elementary School,
Cary, North Carolina

I like writing because then you learn to hold a pencil and to write down something about your story and go over and type and draw in it. That's two of the things to finish it up. The computers were pretty good to me because you got to do computer words, and I know a lot of them. You could put a couple more words around and make a sentence out of them. You could read it over and over again. If you've got a couple of things wrong, you just fix it up. You can make stories and out of sentences.

                                        Writing to Read student

WE KNOW THAT Writing to Read works because we have the living proof. Average children of kindergarten and first grade age have learned to write and to read remarkably well in an amazingly short time in our original experimental classrooms, and currently, more than 100,000 children in hundreds of schools across the country are learning successfully using our method.

But letters of praise like the one above and other indications of progress lead me to believe that the way we're talking, with all this "gee whiz" and "golly" and hoopla, one could easily think that the Writing to Read System works with all the children everywhere and that any child who is exposed to it is going to succeed famously. Well, the program is good but it isn't that good—because nothing is. I want to make clear that we don't have a panacea, the equivalent of the carnival pitchman's elixir that cures rheumatism, takes off warts, and relieves arthritis. Writing to Read isn't magic.

I know there is a need to clarify the limits of the program because of an experience I had about a year ago. I was sitting in the room as a premier marketing representative of IBM made his presentation to the members of a state board of education. He showed some videotapes, talked about the results achieved in the experimental school districts, and was such an enthusiast that the very act of keeping his enthusiasm under control and speaking with decorum and dignity produced an effect much more powerful than if he had waved his arms and shouted, "Come and get the miracle cure for everything that's wrong in the schools."

The people from the board of education sat at a large conference table and around the periphery of the room sat the professionals from that state's department of education—the reading specialists, the language arts people, psychologists, learning theorists, and curriculum planners. The people from the state board of education were nodding their heads and responding affirmatively to the presentation, but I could sense that the professionals were becoming more and more uneasy with what they were hearing. They obviously had healthy doubts about the efficacy of the program.

When I was asked to say a few words I began by saying that, yes, the effects of Writing to Read had proven to be superior to other programs that use standard basal-reading textbooks, but that these effects should be examined critically. First, I cited our data that showed that children in Raleigh, North Carolina, had achieved average scores at the 89th percentile on standardized reading tests in a district that had not previously come within 25 points of that level. Then I pointed to the fact hidden in this remarkable data that 50 percent of the children scored below that level, and within that bottom half as many as 5 percent had achieved very little or no success whatever.

I wanted these professionals to know that while the Writing to Read System went a long way toward curing the learning problems of many children, it clearly worked more effectively with some children than others and it greatly reduced, but didn't eliminate, the percentage of failure. Writing to Read has made a significant contribution toward raising our expectations of what children can learn, but we should learn to seek improvements not miracles.

Continuing, I went on to say that in the course of our work we also seem to have proved that the Writing to Read System speeds up the process of learning to write and read. I wanted to make clear that speed is not, in and of itself, an important goal or even a virtue. We don't need "hurry-up" learning, but when we assembled the factors that make up Writing to Read, each of which contributes a small piece of learning theory, the dynamic interaction of the factors produced, as a by-product, increased speed in learning. More importantly this approach helped children understand the whole idea of what reading and writing are all about. The standard method of teaching young children—those endless months of drill, that constant repetition—confirms its own snail's pace by the poverty of the excitement it brings to the learning act. After all, what is more dreary than the unthinking exercises called for in the primers and their deadly companions, the workbooks designed to keep children quiet?

Yet a series of carefully crafted activities that tends to produce a match between the learner's mental patterns and the thing to be learned frequently produces an electrical spark, an instantaneous response, the "Eureka, I've got it" effect. We've observed this reaction in many, many children but not in all. Nevertheless, it is the highly significant number of children that are successful using the Writing to Read System that makes the program important.

The other point I made to this group grows out of what I've just said. One of the main lessons research teaches us is that the amount we don't know is much greater than what we do know. We have much more to learn. Each new discovery opens a door into a room whose walls have other doors that must be opened if progress is to continue. Today, we know more than we did ten years ago and we will learn more in the years to come. We will surely know more when there is more research into the greatest mystery on earth, the brain, more knowledge about the right and left hemispheres of the brain and the connecting switchboard between the two hemispheres, a precise determination of the role of the hypothalamus and the more primitive elements of the brain, and additional insights into the role of the spinal column, the body's electrochemical processes, and the effects of hormones. All this is being studied with exciting prospects of bringing new insights into how we learn. But each new piece of knowledge is just a small spark that sheds a little light on our progress.

And if we know only a fraction of what we need to know about learning, we may know even less about behavior. We don't know how much power is exerted by the focus of the will of the learner. An example that verges on science fiction comes from Dr. Lewis Thomas, a medical research scientist. The subject is warts and he describes how experiments have shown that the human will can remove a wart. Using hypnotic suggestion patients have, through an unknown mechanism in the brain, removed the warts only on the left sides of their bodies. What is the mechanism? What is the super-brain that can will the proper movement of blood to the capillaries? What are the antibodies that must be mobilized? A brain with this kind of power, which is to say the normal brain, shows mysterious, seemingly limitless potential.

The point of my remarks was to make clear that when we speak about learning to read, learning to write, learning anything, it is important to understand that what we do is a primitive exploration through a mysterious country in which we've scarcely landed on the shore. Right now we have insights, and the little bit we do know—our ideas about how learning occurs, how it is augmented, fertilized, energized, mobilized—is only a faint glimmer on the horizon. Each of these elements, when isolated, is so strong that the discoverers, like the Hindu blind men describing an entire elephant from its parts when they have never seen the whole, have tended to think they have the whole of human learning encompassed in the one part that is being described. Skinner has been, inadvertently, most responsible for this parochial understanding of how learning occurs. His followers have foisted on computer learning a mode of stimulus, response, reward, and punishment (a theory of conditioned learning that is derivative of Pavlov) which is in itself a narrow understanding of how animals and people learn. Still each piece seems so important that the temptation is to say, Now we have it all. We don't have it yet, and what we're describing here will be considered primitive, if we are fortunate, in a few years.

Having said this, I asked for questions from the assembled educators but they had none. I'm sure that I didn't cover the subject completely, and I don't know if this little disclaimer allayed their fears, but it made me feel better to put the case for Writing to Read in a more modest perspective.

It is that perspective I want to convey to the parents who will use this book as a guide in teaching their children. The message is: Writing to Read works, but it isn't the answer for every child and it certainly isn't the whole answer to learning. Use it and discover for yourself if the type of progress we've described is evident in your child. But be patient. The children using the Writing to Read System in the schools use it for at least twenty weeks, and they have the advantage of the computer as well.

# CHAPTER 5

# THE ROLE OF REASON AND LOGIC IN LEARNING: MORE OF THE THEORY BEHIND WRITING TO READ

One dā I went too thu fair. I went on thu cars. I went on thu motersikls. I went on thu moterbots. I went in thu fun house. I was jumping. I loookt in thu mieru. I went in thu hawntid house it was a rīd. it was skeerē it went dinjulling.

I went on thu fastist rīd. I went on a miruhouse. thāir was mirus up stairs I lookd funē. I went on thu yelo slīd. I went on a rolerkoster. I went on thus litl faris whēl. Thin I left.

David, first grade

In Cindergarden yo doo fun stuf. Lik finding noo frinsand my frinds are Dawn Kelli Detru and Shannon and DeAnn. And you lern how to tel tim. And count muny to. And you have sinters. And you hav P.E. and we hav art. We go to the cumpooter room. And at the beginning ov scool you have plan paper and lin paper to. We lisen to recerds. We lisen to storres to. We doo fun work. And we hav rest tim to. And we have happy helpers to. And we have leter pepool. And we lern ouer alforbet. We lrn how to spel culers. And we lern to spel ouer noomrrools.

And we lern about plants. And we get to pant and go to housekeping. And we lern about spas and we lern ol the planets. And we had super kids day and we won two tims and we wer sekent plas and we won therd plas to. And we plad over under and we plad under and plad with the hooler hoops. And we rast to. And now the yier is ol most over.

WHEN THESE CHILDREN wrote their stories on the typewriter, they knew how to talk and they had been taught how to use reason and logic to form words, phrases, and sentences. This represents a complicated mental task, but these children were able to do it and they are typical, normal children.

The roles of reason and logic (the ability to think) in the act of learning are perhaps the most important and at the same time the most misunderstood and neglected areas in all of learning theory. The basic idea is that things are learned when they fit into one of the internal patterns in the brain. One such common brain structure, which I define as a common pattern of thinking, is the universal tendency of young children to attempt to erect towers or roads out of three or more similar objects such as blocks, checkers, or spoons. This tendency, this existing cognitive structure, can be mobilized in learning to write by having a child "see" that a word is a lining up of letters. As you read in the previous chapter, in the Writing to Read System the computer visually assembles a word on the screen by moving letters from their alphabetical order around the edges of the screen to the center of the screen. This is done one letter at a time in step-by-step fashion until the whole word is lined up. This method of presentation fits the very common "lining up" thought pattern in children's brains.

This use of logical structure, a vital part of learning theory, seems easy enough to understand; still, the direct application of the concept to formalized education is difficult to find in the basal-reading textbooks used by the schools. It may sound absurd to say that we pay so little attention to this fundamental principle of learning that we rarely invite children to think in order to learn, but it is nevertheless true.

Yet the language children use to describe their awareness of how they think in order to learn, their use of reason
and logic, resonates with the tones and textures of this
discovery. Here are some of the spontaneous words and
exclamations used by children when they learn: "Now I see
it." "Why didn't you say it that way the first time?" "It's all
coming together now." "So that's the way it goes." "Now it
makes sense."

What these telling phrases indicate is that children are
learning, they are fitting pieces into that great system of
internal patterns, filling in the details in the brain's mosaic.
The different patterns and structures in which the incoming
information must fit are what we're looking for in designing
materials to help learning. When we achieve that pattern
or that match, children exclaim, and adults do too, "Now it
makes sense." Piaget, the great Swiss psychologist, referred
to this process as the assimilation of information into the
existing cognitive structure of the brain. Notice the use of
the revealing word in the statement "Now it fits." A fit, a
match between a brain pattern and the elements to be learned,
constitutes high-quality learning. Now it "makes sense."

Few children can articulate the actual thought processes they have used or are using when they are writing
their first words. Nor will they learn by having these processes preached to them. Thus, it is of little use to tell a
child that a word is a string of letters that stand for the
sounds in the words. If, however, we can have a child see
the visible assembly of a word out of letters moving to form
that word, as we do in the Writing to Read System, the idea
becomes real, real enough for that child to "make words" in
the same manner—piecing them together a letter at a time.
So having learned in the very first lesson by seeing how the
computer writes the words *cat, dog,* and *fish,* the child is
tutored by the computer into typing the words *fat, fog,* and
*dish.* These new words are formed a letter at a time from
the letters used in the words *cat, dog,* and *fish.* By very
deliberate emphasis this process is repeated in each of the
ten cycles on the computer and in the accompanying Work
Journals. With three words in each cycle, the ten cycles

contain thirty words, which in turn contain the forty-two phonemes, the letters and letter combinations which represent all the sounds used in speaking English. This repetition communicates to the learning child how spoken words can be made visible by writing the letters that stand for the sounds in those words. Children, therefore, learn by thinking "What sound comes next?" Once a child has learned to do this, to ask "What sound comes next?" and then to ask himself what letter or letters stand for that sound, he has made a gigantic intellectual leap toward learning to write and then to read.

In the act of learning to write and to read, we encourage this basic human intellectual drive to look for and find patterns and structures. We show children how to match their mental patterns, the way they think, to new structures, called words, by providing the missing connections to the concept to be learned. One way to understand what may be happening is to think of one transparency being put down as an overlay on top of another. That's what the Writing to Read System tries to do.

Another teaching concept of the Writing to Read System can also be simply stated. We believe that writing is a more powerful act than reading because it is ego centered and gives an outlet to a child's natural urge to speak on paper. A child who writes will surely learn to read, but it is not a certainty that a child that learns to read will learn to write. The proof of this is the fact that our high schools and colleges are full of students who cannot write a coherent paragraph.

Writing to Read exploits the natural learning potential of children and it exploits the educational potential of computer technology. It does this from an historical perspective that takes into account the way in which literacy is taught in our culture, and at the same time draws on various and diverse theories of the learning process.

Natural learning potential, computers, and learning theories aside, how can writing motivate children to learn to read if, as most educators have espoused for decades, a child must first learn to read in order to learn to write. The answer requires that the question be turned around, and in turning it, we need to look more closely at the nature of learning, at phonemics and language, at computers and curriculum.

For the Writing to Read System to work, one important prerequisite must be met: The child must be able to grasp the idea that the alphabet stands for sounds, and that the words he or she hears and speaks are the very same sounds assembled to form words. If a child can catch this seemingly simple idea, then writing becomes a logical process of putting down an order of sounds in visual form.

The story of one of our students, whom I'll call William, illustrates the power of this concept. William was a gentle boy whose IQ of 55 indicated that he was a mentally retarded, educable student. He had been held back in both kindergarten and first grade because he could not seem to learn. Already nine years old when he came to the Writing to Read laboratory, he had yet to write his first word, and even drawing his name was a struggle. Of course, he wasn't able to read and he had a speaking vocabulary of no more than 125 words. He was also extremely passive and easy to overlook because he was not yet a discipline problem.

One day, we found William at a laboratory table on the three sides of which were displayed the forty-two plastic plates that contained all the graphemes we used in the classroom. He was alone, so one of the staff members sat down next to him and quietly explained that since she knew that he could recognize all the sounds on the grapheme plates she was certain he could write words. William made a very dubious face. "I can?" he asked. The instructor assured him that he could and pressed on by asking him what he would like to write about. It was February and the first president's birthday was being studied in class, so William said he would like to write about George Washington. After some urging he began, and he slowly and laboriously wrote:

Gorg Washingtun, I hōp you hav a loving burthday and th tēcher hōps you hav a loving burthday.
William

It took almost thirty minutes to get this short message down on paper because he did it slowly, a phoneme at a time. He had finally grasped the idea. And believe it or not, from that day on, relative to his maturity level, William made measurable, discernible, and continuous progress. For example, in two weeks William wrote the following underneath a picture cut from an old magazine:

## The Cheetah

The Cheetah is the fastis animial in the world. The Cheetah cachiz smal animalz. the Cheetah is cleen. the Cheetah washes his fās when he eats. The end. William

The concept that William finally grasped—that the alphabet stands for sounds, and that words we can speak are the same words we see when they are written with letters—is easier to conceive than to accomplish. The reason is that the construction of the English language itself makes the understanding of this principle a difficult proposition. Over its long history, English has gone through many changes, and the rules for English spelling are complex and unreliable. Therefore, it is difficult to fix the relationship between graphemes (the visual letters) and phonemes (the sounds of those letters) without such frequent exceptions to the rules that young learners become confused.

We are very fond of teaching children the rule that when single syllable words end in *e*, the first vowel says its name, as in *home* and *stove* and *cave* and *five*; but rarely do we help children with such common exceptions as *come, love, move,* and *give*. The alphabetic inconsistencies and spelling irregularities of English have been recognized for 400 years. We pronounce many words differently now than we did then, but we continue to spell them in the old way. As our pronunciation has changed, we have tended to leave the spelling unchanged. To write the way we speak now is to misspell many words.

It's been twenty-five years since linguist Leonard Bloomfield made a plaintive plea to educators to make use of the maximum phonemic regularity available in English to teach reading. He wrote: "Our teaching ought to distinguish, then, between *regular* spellings which involve only the alphabetic principle, and *irregular* spellings which depart from this principle, and it ought to classify the irregular spellings according to the various types of derivation from the alphabetic principle."

A promising idea and a helpful piece of clarification, but the question remained: Is the limited degree of regularity in conventional English sufficient to offer support to students and to offset confusion over the exceptions? These special problems of grapheme-phoneme agreement, or more accurately lack of agreement, have inspired some ingenious approaches to the teaching of reading.

One of these, devised by Caleb Gattegno, is called Words in Color. In his system the phonemes are color coded so that appropriately coded writing can be pronounced correctly on the basis of the color of the letters. This means that the color system must be learned and then unlearned as the child gains skill in reading. Nevertheless, Gattegno achieved impressive results. Sir James Pitman used an alternative approach with the same goal. His Initial Teaching Alphabet used a new alphabet constructed to provide a single grapheme for each of the forty-two sounds of spoken English. But as with Words in Color, Pitman's alphabet had to be discarded in the transition period when a child begins to learn the way words are really spelled. Again, several studies reported improved reading scores.

If by chance a child has learned to read and write without the use of color codes or a special alphabet, there has been, until now, no alternative to early and often discouraging encounters with the vast array of rules, exceptions, and arbitrary differences that must be learned in order to relate groups of letters to their sounds. Yet despite these obstacles, Jeanne Chall summarized the research which found that an early emphasis on phonics was the most effective way to learn to read.

This being the case, it might seem hopeless to ask a

child to write words when he is in the throes of the initial struggle with beginning reading. He would want to write words that are in his speaking vocabulary—more than 2,000 words for an average child—but that have not yet been encountered in reading. The child would either have very little idea of how to write such a word or, more than likely, have the wrong idea. For this reason, the power of writing as a motivator for all language behavior has remained largely unexploited despite Maria Montessori's advocacy of writing before reading more than eighty years ago and the more recent work of the Spaldings along the same lines. (And I. A. Richards pointed out that Chall had neglected, in her review of the research, the role of early writing as a means of teaching reading.)

Removal of phonemic difficulties also makes it possible to remove another roadblock that has been placed in front of children. Carol Chomsky has shown that the developing urge to write can be encouraged if the child is released from the choking inhibitions of having to try to spell correctly. She found that children can grasp the essence of the alphabetic principle and invent spelling appropriate to their phonemic understanding and skill with remarkable ease. In fact, few of the writing examples in this book would have been possible if Writing to Read demanded correct spelling.

In summary, we find:

- An English alphabet whose application to the spelling of words has nearly as many exceptions as it has hard and fast rules
- A number of alternative systems that have not been able to achieve lasting application over the long run
- A variety of phonics systems that work better than the "whole word" or "look-say" process but which continue to produce an unacceptable rate of failure
- .Research which shows that children can learn to write in superior fashion more easily if they don't have to worry about spelling in the initial stages of learning.

We have taken these facts into consideration in the research and development of Writing to Read, and the knowledge we have gleaned from them now serves as the foundation of the system. Writing to Read provides a set of
activities that help children understand that what they *say*,
they can *write*. They learn the logic of listening to the sounds
in their words, and they learn to write the commonly used
alphabetic symbols for those sounds. In doing this they are
able to write all the words that they can say.

No new letters or letter combinations are used in the
Writing to Read System. The alphabet used to help children
understand the relationship between the letters and their
relatively consistent sounds is derived from the most agreed
upon common dictionary pronunciation keys, and while these
pronunciation keys differ from one dictionary to the other,
their similarities are the basis for the simplified alphabet
used in Writing to Read. As a pleasant by-product, our children have a head start in learning how to use the dictionary
to find the proper pronunciation of words.

After all this discussion about the various pitfalls involved in devising a workable system, you may be asking
yourself if our simplified alphabet can actually help children
write English with all its irregularities. The answer is an
emphatic yes.

The alphabet we have developed is derived from the
work of Godfrey Dewey. Dewey's scholarship discovered
the more than 500 ways commonly used to spell the forty-
two sounds in spoken English. He subsequently produced
an alphabet called World English Spelling, or WES. The
grapheme-phoneme relationships in WES are adequate
without creating new letters or combinations of letters, though
Dewey used the letter *e* following a vowel to designate the
long vowel sound. He did this in order to meet the criteria
established by spelling reform linguists who felt that eliminating the diacritical marks used in dictionaries to aid
pronunciation would make for a more rational and easier-
to-pronounce alphabet.

A guiding principle of the Writing to Read System, which
we adopted from Dewey, is to reduce the irregularities and

uncertainties faced by children at the very beginning stages of writing—with the idea that this would free them to learn.

Our departure from Dewey's alphabet began with our practical application of the system in the classroom. We quickly learned to accept children's spelling. We accepted any spelling which made phonemic sense. For example, the pronoun *you* may be spelled "yoo." But "yū," with the macron bar (hard sound) above the *u,* or simply the long vowel *u* standing by itself accomplishes the same result. We ended up using the macron for long vowel sounds and found that children responded well. We eliminated Dewey's awkward-appearing *e* to designate the long vowels and found that this also offered no difficulties for children.

We also wanted to reduce the discrepancy between our temporary learning alphabet and conventional spelling, so we dropped the diphthongs *aa* as in *father* and *uu* as in the sound of *oo* in *book*. The short vowel *o* as in *bother* takes care of the first, and the use of *oo* to represent the sound in both *school* and *book* (conventional spelling) has not caused any difficulties except with purists who find our pragmatism to be inconsistent. We also use *air* for the many spellings for that common phoneme. In the end we came up with the list of forty-two phonemes you saw in chapter 2. Here they are again:

| | | | |
|---|---|---|---|
| a | c | d | f | g |
| i | o | t | sh | b |
| e | n | p | s | u |
| l | r | th | ē | k |
| m | v | ā | h | j |
| w | y | ī | ar | oo |
| z | ō | au | er | ou |
| ur | air | ch | wh | |
| oi | or | ū | | |

We teach the children to write these sounds using an illustrative word drawn from their common speech. This demonstrates the principle very directly and shows how the sounds are made from the letters and combinations of letters of the alphabet. The thirty words that contain these forty-two phonemes are:

> cat  dog  fish  pig  sun  bed
> rabbit  leg  thrē  man  snāk
> vās  jump  hand  wagon  yard
> moon  kīt  zipper  straw  smōk
> turtl  chair  hous  oil  hors
> whēl  ūniform  book  butter

These words were carefully selected from children's oral vocabularies to fulfill several criteria, but most importantly, they were chosen because they embody a regular set of agreements between the forty-two phonemes and the look of ordinary English words as they are conventionally spelled. When children learn these agreements, they quickly can write almost any word they can think of or say, even though they may spell it incorrectly.

The advantage of seeing and spelling words by the alphabet-phoneme method, not always in conformity with usage, has disadvantages of brief duration, but an enormous advantage in the long term. There wouldn't be much need to mention this except for the compulsiveness of parents and teachers regarding correct spelling, a compulsiveness that has little to do either with the intellectual growth of children or with their mastery of the language. My personal feeling is that it may well be this insistence on correct spelling in the early stages of a youngster's attempts at writing that is one cause of our adult population's inhibitions about writing and their general inability to write with skill.

Please don't get the idea from this that we are opposed to correct spelling. Writing to Read encourages children to adopt conventional spelling as soon as they recognize the alternatives they see in books, what we call the "book way" of spelling. So, for example, when a child writes *I* as *i*, it isn't long before the use of the capital *I* is adopted. Surprisingly, many children begin making the transition to conventional spelling from the very first moment they gain an insight into how to write. The phonemic alphabet, as we've devised it, is only a temporary tool that children find useful in writing what they want to say. They seem to be able to lay it aside quite naturally as they encounter and accept conventional spelling.

It's been interesting to note throughout the development of Writing to Read that children can quite readily accept a certain amount of ambiguity, provided it appears in a rational context. If they think the whole learning task is sensible, then minor aberrations can be accepted without confusion, frustration, or rebellion. Their learning doesn't seem to require absolutes; reasonable symmetry will do. Would that some of the rigid adult personalities we encounter could tolerate as comfortably the minor accommodations we find so necessary for everyday living.

This fact was brought home to me strongly while observing one of our experimental classes in a school in Stuart, Florida. I was moving down a row of children hard at work hunting and pecking out their stories on the typewriter. I looked over one boy's shoulder and could see that of the seventy-five or so words on his paper many were spelled conventionally, including *have* and *save,* which have a silent *e.* This indicated to me that he knew what he was doing in shifting from phonemic to conventional spelling.

Looking more closely, however, I saw that he had twice written the word "wuns" for *once.* Since we made it a practice not to correct but to ask what it was the child was trying to say, I tapped him on the shoulder to get his attention. With that "hurrumphing" sort of irritation children show when their deep concentration is interrupted, he turned with a frown to find out who was bothering him. Without saying a word, he asked with a facial expression, "What do *you* want?" I pointed to the twice-written word "wuns" and said, "What's that word, Frankie? I can't read it." He answered quickly, "That's *once.*" And then, as a smile covered his face, he added, "Would you like 'on-ke' better?" It was obvious that not only did he know what he was doing but he had put himself on top of the idiosyncrasies of English spelling and was enjoying it. His humor revealed his sense of personal pride in his spelling.

You will recall our earlier discussion of the importance of applying Piaget's concept of children's learning through their matching "cognitive structures" to the task they face. Our young typist writing "wuns" demonstrated another application of Piaget coupled with Bruner's insights. Bruner speaks of well-developed "subject-matters" and of school learning as "learning designed to produce general understanding of the structure of a subject-matter." He goes on to say that "a theory of instruction must specify the ways in which a body of knowledge should be structured so that it can be most readily grasped by the learner." For him, the merits of a structure depend on its power to simplify information, to generate new ideas, and to increase the manipulatability of a body of information. He points out that the internal logic of a subject is critical. So while Bruner is speaking of the large structure of a subject such as biology or reading, Piaget is speaking of the structure or patterns of thinking already formed in a learner's brain. Our task, whose success is so well illustrated by the boy typist, was to bring those two structures together. What we sought was the mental equivalent of putting one pattern on top of another to find an approximate match. In this case the phonemic values of our alphabet (Bruner's subject structure) in writing a word meshed with the boy's insistence on making sense out of his writing a word (Piaget's cognitive structure).

As we have said, learning occurs when a child's mind absorbs new information and is modified by that learning. But we can't see into a child's mind, so we can only infer the existence of mental structures by the observation of recurring patterns in the behavior of children. As I've said, one such persistent pattern that is characteristic of four- and five-year-olds is their tendency to put three or more similar objects in a column or in a row. Part of our job, as curriculum and software designers, was to look into the nature of the thing to be learned and find what there was in that material that lent itself to being understood by matching the cognitive structure that calls for putting things in a line.

A word in print is an assembly of letters, things in a row, a row of sounds that when spoken become the word; a row of letters which, when written in the order they are spoken, make that word visible. As the letters or the letter pairs are typed, they leave their "homes" on the edge of the computer monitor screen where they have been sitting in an alphabetic row, and march out to take up positions in a new row in the center of the computer screen. The letters in their home rows are always in the same alphabetical position, but in words, of course, the positions they take depend on the word.

We think that in our approach the two types of structures reinforce each other, that the rational aspect of phonemic spelling connects with the cognitive structures in children's mental processes. By adopting the computer's ability to use moving graphics, Writing to Read makes visible the lining up of letters to make a word and satisfies the mental inclination to put things in a row.

We have tried to put these principles of reason and logic into every aspect of Writing to Read. Our work has evolved over many years, adding a piece at a time, an element here with this child, an action there with another child, reshaping, redrawing, retesting, redesigning, and always watching the reactions of one child at a time. Out of this work came the design of the Writing to Read System—the role of the computer, the use of the typewriter, the sensory-oriented materials, and the Work Journals. These elements are discussed in the following chapters.

# CHAPTER 6

# MULTI-SENSORY PERCEPTION

a rabbit

One time i wanted a rabbit then he wus mi pet he wus mi vere best fren and he nibld u hol in mi shert then he nibld mi bruthers shert he did not lik the sherts so he at sum carits aftr that he wus ful.

Once I was walking in the woods. Oh! No! I saw a bear. I took him home. He got me dirty. So I took a bath. he got in there with me. I said Oh! Me! I got out and dryed off Then I went to wathch T.V. he sat in my lap and he smild. So I went to bed he sleped with me. I said Give me a break. It was finaly morning. I took him back. he folowd me home. I said I'll just have to live with him!

GIVE A SMALL child a soft rabbit, a teddy bear, an animal cracker, or a hard cookie and watch the complete sensory examination of the object. The child looks at it closely with his eyes; he feels it with his fingers and rubs it against other parts of his body; he sniffs it with his nose, places it against his lips, licks it with his tongue, murmurs sounds or words, and finally puts it in his mouth for the ultimate test. This is complete multi-sensory perception.

If we think of the human brain as a processing center, a magnificent supercomputer that gathers, assimilates, manipulates, and distributes data, the means by which information is sent to the central processing unit of the brain computer are the five senses. The human organism acts like an octopus with five tentacles, gathering information from a variety of different sources at the same time. Every milli-second the body relays bits of information to the brain, in-formation which is being absorbed through the eyes, the ears, and the senses of smell, taste, and feel.

The research on multi-sensory perception dates back at least 100 years and its findings are significant for the Writing to Read program. The research has clearly shown that when tasks are designed to appeal to many senses at the same time children (and adults for that matter) learn more quickly.

Take a moment to try your own sensory experiment. Close your eyes and have someone give you an object to hold in your hands. The object has a distinctive feel of smooth-ness or roughness or softness, and you can sense its weight. It smells sweet or sour, mild or strong, or not at all. If you tap it, it makes a sound that tells you if it is solid or hollow or somewhere in between. Put it to your lips and it tastes sweet, sour, mild, or strong, and the tastes on your tongue are confirmed by the nose. All of this information is contin-uously passed on to the brain, which makes running cal-culations and then gives you a decision on the identity of the object. You can then open your eyes to confirm the brain's appraisal, and you will see the object's color and its shape and you'll identify it with a word.

In the same way that most of your senses were engaged in your sensory experiment, the Writing to Read System engages many of a young child's information-gathering senses at the same time. All of the materials placed in front of the learner are designed to evoke a multi-sensory un-derstanding of their nature, of their substance, so that they will be understood more readily and more completely. We involve the eyes, the ears, and the sense of touch and smell through the use of clay, chalk, sand, pencil, typewriter, and computer. Would that we could persuade a cookie company to bake very hard, sweet-tasting cookies with a pleasant aroma that have the shape of the letters of the alphabet so children could use their tongues to feel and taste the letter *a* while the delightful smell fills their noses. In the Hebrew Talmud the commentaries include advice to the teachers of the beginning reader to hold a pot of honey ready so that when a child reads his first word, the tutor can dip his finger in the honey and place it on the lips of the child, so that "forever after learning shall be sweet in the memory of the child."

Maria Montessori, the Italian teacher who opened schools in the slums of Rome more than eighty years ago, was one of the pioneers in the multi-sensory approach to learning. She called her school the Children's House, and it was filled with learning materials that she called "didactic apparatus." The "form-boards" she developed are a good example of her technique. Today, they are a familiar item to every new parent as those "toys" with squares, triangles, circles, rectangles, stars, and other shapes that fit into only one spot in pre-cut sections of a board. Montessori's form-boards were not designed as toys at all but as toylike devices that simulated objects used in the adult world. They weren't exact replicas but they resembled workaday objects in some key properties, and a child's manipulation of these devices developed skills that were useful in the urban industrial world of Montessori's clientele. In her writing she speaks of "didactic material for the education of the senses," of "didactic material for preparation for writing and arithmetic," and of "didactic material for motor education."

Didactic material is an accurate and telling term. The form-board is interesting and complex in its simplicity because it can "tell" whether the correct shape has been placed against a recess on the board. It does this by either accepting or rejecting the shape, and the child working with the shape immediately knows if he is right or wrong. Both perceptual and motor skills are needed in order to make the match. The "right" shape must also be placed in the right angular position as well, and this is an additional skill that is useful in the development of eye-hand coordination. Montessori invented all of her own learning aids, including the use of fine-textured sandpaper cut in the shape of letters so children could get the feel of the letter at the same time they were seeing the shape. An important element of didactic material is its self-corrective construction so children can see without adult confirmation that they are successful.

Once asked to explain the key principle of her method

of teaching, Montessori described it as "liberty in a prepared environment," and she said: "The whole history of civilization is a history of successful attempts to organize work and obtain liberty." Clearly a person of vision, Montessori had another theme of great power, and that was her reliance on the natural reinforcement children developed in actually "running the house," actually directing and pacing themselves in many ways. Today, this theme of "self-actualization" and "self-pacing" is more often echoed in the halls of education than it is implemented.

Writing to Read has adapted many of the findings of Montessori. Our materials (chalk, slate, sand, clay), the computer, and the typewriter are designed to be didactic. Our environment is prepared, our work organized, and the children just about "run the house." Of course, there is adult supervision—and we take special care around the instructional diskettes because they are sensitive to peanut butter and sticky fingers—but otherwise, a child in the program moves at his own pace, visits the learning station of his choice, stays as long as he wants within limits, and does what the prepared material invites him to do.

So we know that children take in information through their senses, not only the senses of sight and hearing, which enjoy special status in formal education, but through all of their senses. If instructional information is available in many sensory areas at the same time, a child is more likely to find a match which suits his or her unique disposition. That's why the Writing to Read computers speak and the children are asked to clap, sing, and stamp their feet. And all the listening and writing stations in the Writing to Read laboratory are equipped with a variety of sense-stimulating devices.

But the importance of the multi-sensory capability is probably not restricted to the production of rich textures, which send the same message in differing ways, inundate with redundancy, and accommodate individual differences in learning style. Stimuli other than speech and print are needed to bring new behavior into relationships with the properties of the world. Such properties as shape, color, and motion are good examples, though color identification should be separated from learning to read. All reading is in black and white, and at least 5 percent of all boys are unidentified color-blind. Teachers using conventional materials supplied by textbook publishers routinely attempt to drill these color-blind boys in matching colored balloons, and they succeed only in teaching them that they are destined to have trouble learning to read. In the same way, a phoneme-grapheme must be heard and seen, seen and heard, heard and seen, not merely heard *or* seen, in order to build the ability to discriminate between them as they occur in words drawn from children's speech. Making letters out of clay, with a finger in sand or Jell-O powder, pencil on paper, and chalk on slate are reinforcements designed to bring children's writing, their recall, to the level of an automatic response.

Children differ widely in the way in which they gather information from their senses, just as they differ in the way they mobilize one sense over another. A child's sensory print is as distinctive as his or her fingerprint. Some children respond more readily to things they see, some to things they hear, and so forth. At the same time, they are able to shift the emphasis of their senses in the same way adults do. For example, people often shut their eyes when listening to music and allow their ears to do the perceiving. In the same way we rely on the senses of smell and taste when eating, and we trust the sense of touch in a darkened room. The point is, all the senses are critical to the learning process, and the more senses that can be brought to bear on a task, the more choices a child has and the more quickly the task will be accomplished.

What this means is that learning materials must be organized with enough diversity to present a cafeteria of sensory opportunities to every learner and, at the same time, provide everyone with a chance to grasp the concept of what is to be learned. Children need to be free to select for themselves those materials they are intuitively comfortable with. Thus some will not be repeatedly attracted to the sand tray, others will be drawn often to the clay, and still others will change from day to day. Each child must have this freedom of choice. This is one case where adults do not know best.

Our emphasis, drawn from Piaget, in these beginning stages is based on the fact that in the early years learning is a series of sensory-motor experiences. Introducing the learning of letters, sounds, and words through as many senses as possible reinforces children as they mature and move to the concrete level of their development.

## CHAPTER 7

# SOME ADDITIONAL KEYS TO SUCCESSFUL LEARNING

### Billy

Mī nām is Billy. Mī hous number is 59. Mī heāir is blond. I am six yers old. Mī īz ar bloo. I have three siders debe barbara and didi. I hav 5 bruthers jarē chris and john mīk and ed. Mī momē name is mairrē loo. Mi favoerit tv sho is hot potato i līk to git the wus bfoer. i līk sal uv the senters. I wont to be a polēsman when i grō up. I wont to do trafik signals. I wont to arest pēpl.

I līk the computer room becos we go to the computers writing sinter and the typewriters to and the gām and the book sinter. Thin we rēd a storē. Thin we tāc a nap. Thin whin we wāc up we ēt snac. Thin we will go out sīd. Thin we will cum in to hav shō and tel. Thin we will rēd a short storē.

LIKE A DIAMOND which shows new facets as it is turned and examined under the jeweler's loupe, the diamond we call learning has many facets. Some, like the alphabetic principle and the phonemic alphabet, are sharply defined and they readily catch the eye with their critical importance. Other facets are less apparent because they are more subtle; yet they are also critical to the process of learning, and if they are neglected, the sparkle and brilliance of the whole is diminished.

Three of the more subtle elements that make learning easier and better are:

- *Self-direction,* a measure of control over what you do when you are learning
- *Evidence* of learning, which we call by the computer-age term "hard copy"
- *Mastery* of the subject matter, knowing that you know.

## SELF-DIRECTION

Self-actualization and self-realization were two of the more creative buzz words of the 1970s. Because of the changing manners and mores of those years, the two terms were surrounded by a mystique far out of proportion to their hazy meaning. They became symbols for an age that talked of "doing your own thing" and making "life-style changes," but what they actually inferred was being "in charge," or more grandly, "determining your own destiny." According to the conventional wisdom of those years, acquiring this powerful feeling of self-determination could transform the average person into an aggressive but not abusive, self-confident but not egotistical person who was content within himself and with other people.

All the trumpeting aside, if these words are removed from the faddish excesses they represented in the context of the 1970s, self-directing adults are healthier people than those poor souls pulled in all directions by varying fads. The important thing to realize, however, is that this is not just a character trait to be learned as an adult. Children who learn, while they are learning other skills, that they are in charge of themselves, in charge of their own learning, are really growing in maturity as well. This is double learning indeed.

Therefore, we designed Writing to Read activities so that each child is invited to be in charge. A child who can see and direct the series of actions involved in the learning activity is a child who will learn rapidly. In contrast, a child under the moment-to-moment direction of an adult begins to exhibit a sad form of behavior, an excessive dependence that finds the child continually looking up at the adult and asking, either with a quizzical facial expression or verbally, "Is this right?" and "What do I do next, teacher?" Of course, this isn't a problem that is confined to the schools. Many parents are so directive in the home and outside it that a child is given no latitude to make choices or decisions even on the simplest of matters. If a parent constantly tells a child what to wear, what and how much to eat and drink, when to talk and when to be quiet, even when to go to the bathroom, the child may become trained, submissive, and dependent, or periodically antagonistic and rebellious. Later, this overly submissive or fractious child will be unable to make either the decisions or accommodations required of teenagers and adults.

Thus, self-direction became an integral part of our program from the beginning. The material is so designed that the sequence of actions necessary to complete a task readily becomes apparent, and the series of steps built into the structure of the material is sufficient and consistent enough for the child to respond without adult intervention once the general pattern has been learned. For most children this self-managing routine comes quickly. For others the task is more lengthy. In the first illustration, the earphones tell the child to use the tape and the voice then instructs the child to write the indicated letters, and finally, the whole word.

In the next example you'll note how the page itself teaches and directs. The pictured drawing of a hand holding a pencil tells the child how the page is to be used. The remaining exercises in the Work Journal are also designed to be self-instructive.

The drawing of the upraised hand in the bottom right-hand corner of the last page (see p. 76) is a signal. Children are instructed that when they reach that signal on the page they are to raise their hand so that their teacher can review their progress and so that they can then move on to the next step. This isn't direction as much as it is the periodic

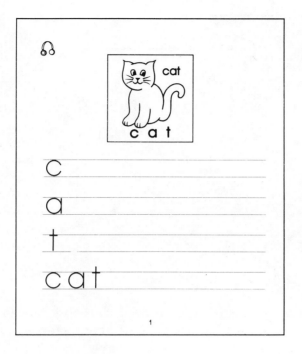

c

a

t

cat

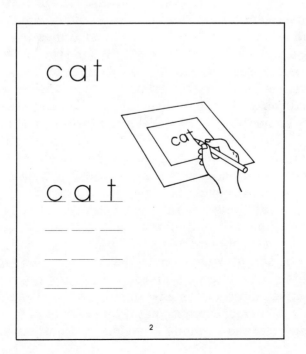

cat

c a t

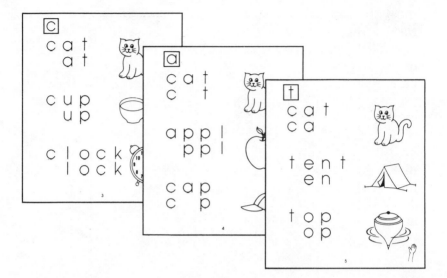

reassurance that children do need. Our task was to insert sufficient guides and directions without fostering a feeling of domination, which can be stultifying.

Why is this so important? Because it produces in the learner the sense that "I am the master of my own destiny," and the feeling of self-satisfaction that comes from being able to say, "I did it myself" and "I finished the job and now I can go on to the next one." This feeling is an empowering force that is good for the ego and for the child's sense of personal worth. In the adult world we certainly recognize that the same thing is true. Given the chance to accomplish a task by ourselves, we thrive. When performing the same job under the yoke of a taskmaster, we can elect to wilt or to revolt. Children should not be confronted with such a devil's choice by a badly designed learning task.

For a child, this provision for independence goes to the heart of the matter and eliminates the need for continual and excessive submission to the will of an adult, either teacher or parent, which can be demeaning in and of itself and which, more often than not, produces the reverse of all the positive conditions just mentioned. That is: The constant dependence on and submission to adult authority in a learning situation (and in many other daily situations as well) most frequently engenders feelings of inadequacy, uncertainty, and powerlessness in a child.

There are a number of techniques to cultivate this self-direction process that we have found useful in the classroom and which are useful for parents too. In the experimental phase of Writing to Read and in practice with thousands of children in schools around the country, we developed a system of internal controls that fosters a child's sense of where he is ultimately headed. We have created a type of map that indicates his location in the program and where he goes next. This map is printed on the back of each of the Work Journals in the form of a series of boxes listing "Computer" and "Work Journal" tasks that must be completed before moving on to the next step.

It is this back cover of the Work Journal that shows the ongoing record of the child's achievement. For example, children mark the square next to the word *cat* when they finish with the word on the computer, and then again when they finish it in the journal. This record of what they're doing is explicitly visual to them as they move on to the Make Words game, to use the typewriter, and to listen to recorded stories. The journal serves as a passport from learning station to learning station, from country to country, if you will, and when the child finishes a visit he gives himself a visa stamp from that part of the learning world. The important thing is that the actual marking of the visa stamp is done, must be done in fact, by the child.

It's important to emphasize this last point. The child's box marks are the important thing. We have found in and outside the classroom that there is a strong adult need to become the keeper of the knowledge gate. More often than not this means taking the pencil from the child and filling in the square which says a task has been completed. I've seen it happen too often. A teacher sees a child finishing a job and rushes to mark the child's progress for him. This obviously isn't done with malice but it successfully destroys the dynamic in a child's learning which says, "If I keep my own record of my work I'll learn better." This is a difficult concept for adults to grasp and even more difficult to accept because it violates the desire to be in charge of our children,

| name_____ | **1** | |
| --- | --- | --- |

| 🖥 computer | | 📖 work journal | |
| --- | --- | --- | --- |
| 1. cat | X | 1. cat | X |
| 2. dog | X | 2. dog | |
| 3. fish | X | 3. fish | X |
| 4. test | X | 4. test | |
| 5. make words | X | 5. make words | |

| make words game | | | |
| --- | --- | --- | --- |
| typewriter | | | |
| listen to stories | | | |

teacher's comments:

work completed _____
                              teacher signature

to keep them dependent, and to show them that they need us. Learn to take pride in their growing independence. They will need you long enough.

Not to overstate the case, children will most certainly learn in spite of this adult intrusion, but as with each of the learning principles in this total learning package, its violation will reduce the effectiveness of a child's learning.

This same type of journal system works equally well in the home with learning or other tasks, though it can certainly be less formalized if the parent wishes. At home the child will get up from the place where he or she works and take his work to you. You can then acknowledge the recording made by the child to map this progress. If the work indicated by the filled-in box is completed in good fashion, the child is free to move to the next activity. If the parent's review indicates the child doesn't quite grasp the material, then the child can be asked to do the work again. This should go on, though not necessarily in one session, until the parent is satisfied that the child has some grasp of the material.

There is another aspect to self-direction that deserves mention and which also has application for the child working at home as well as at school. In the Writing to Read center the children have a sense of ownership, a feeling that the room is their place. They move around it with an assurance that implies comfort and control. Visitors often remark on the behavior of the children as they unconsciously display this sense of ownership by walking with a certain strut. We like to say that "our children walk with square shoulders," which to us means that they move their bodies in a self-assured manner. We feel this is not only a result of the design of the total program but also because there is no one between the child and the learning materials; children actually sense that they have taught themselves. Their pride shows.

In the conventional classroom the teacher acts as a catalytic agent and an explainer. The teacher's role is one of a shower, a teller, a helper, a person who directs and corrects and sometimes scolds. It is implicit in the structure of most of our schools that a book and a child are too seldom left alone. In fact, when we think about it, a child and any task are seldom left alone at school or at home.

In the Writing to Read center, the children work in pairs and are encouraged to help each other at the computer. The learners and the machine are in a structured dialogue. They interact. The computer and the child respond to each other (with as little teacher involvement as possible) and change what they do, at least partially, depending on what one does to the other.

From our point of view this relationship is a positive one, but there are those who have already sounded an alarm against this one-to-one relationship between child and computer because they are fearful that computers have too much "control" over children, that the machine has a mesmerizing effect that is more powerful than the child's ability to resist, and that the machine masters the learner, not the other way around. We've found that, on the contrary, a child does not anthropomorphize the computer. We've made a conscious effort in our program not to give the machine the sugar gloss of falsely human-type qualities such as large

screen graphics saying "GREAT" and "YOU WIN" with fire-
works and noises. We have taken care to avoid the artificial
and shallow language, the so-called "human" touches, that
some computer programs have borrowed from the arcade
games. We have rejected the use of computer-created responses that flash messages on the screen such as, "Hi, Joey,
glad to see you today" or "Good morning, Betty, I hope you
have a good day" or "That's not quite right, Timmy, try
again." We feel these little accommodations, these cute and
facile computer tricks, are a denigration, distracting put-
downs, that even five-year-olds readily recognize simply because they know better. They know this robotic device is
not able to think and that the personalized language is false.
Hence, the gamelike attractions of Writing to Read are intrinsic. They are built into the structure of the exercise.
External patches of flashing graphics and scorekeeping
competitions are artificial icing on stale cake.

The proof of the ability of children to keep the machine
in perspective is illustrated by two incidents. Periodically
during the course of a computer session with Writing to
Read, the computer has to stop and pick new information
off the program diskette to add to its memory. This takes
a few seconds, and since we know that it is difficult for
children to handle an empty screen for more than a few
seconds, we display all the phonemes during this brief hia-
tus and show the blinking word "Thinking" in the middle
of the screen. It's a little joke that children seem to appre-
ciate. We have previously explained to them that the computer has a tiny brain and every so often runs out of what
it needs to remember, and that therefore it must take information off the diskettes while we have to wait.

One day I happened to be watching two little girls as
they sat quietly during this computer "thinking" process.
Both of them were listening to the noise of the disk drive
mechanism, a vaguely rasping sound. With a laugh, one
suddenly turned to the other and said, "Listen, now it's
scratching its head." This child's laughter clearly demonstrated that even at five years of age she had no illusions
about the human characteristics of the computer.

On another occasion a very bright child called to me

from across the room and when I got to his chair he said, "You're right." I said, "Right about what?" "This thing [he pointed at the computer] is dumb," he said. "Oh," I answered, "how did you figure that out?" He said, "Listen, it's going to tell me to say fish." As we listened, the computer said, "Say fish." The youngster responded, "Dog," and then said, "See, it didn't know I said dog." Of course, the machine didn't know what the child said and the child was not fooled into thinking that it did.

Children are perceptive about this sort of thing. They don't deal with the computer as a disembodied spirit with a mind of its own. They know it's a machine and that they are in control.

In summary, what we've created in Writing to Read is the kind of self-direction that gives children the feeling they are teaching themselves, which, in fact, they are. This is ennobling, a vitamin tablet for the spirit. It makes youngsters feel good about themselves, feel that they "can do it" just like the little engine that could. This growing sense of inner competence is extraordinarily important in the healthy development of children. The inner urge to manage their own world is a very strong drive and it should be nurtured.


## EVIDENCE, HARD COPY

Learning is an abstract act, an act that takes place in the recesses of the neurological system. It's very difficult to document and impossible to describe all the processes that result in learning with any degree of certainty. For example, a child can read a word, reread it, and finally learn it (not to be confused with memorization), but it's only when that word is written in context that there is solid evidence that learning has taken place, evidence that the child has done something beyond copying a string of letters on a piece of paper.

Moving from the abstract thought in one's mind to the visibly concrete—this hard copy, as it has come to be called in the computer age—is certain evidence of learning. A child can walk around with information in his head, but without the hard copy, the piece of paper held in the hand, neither the child nor adult can know that something has been learned. This copy is more than evidence of learning, for we have found that the child's holding his writing in his hand is an important personal reinforcement of acquiring knowledge.

In the program, four- and five-year-olds get visible evidence of learning by writing on a slate with chalk. This exercise allows them to examine the shape and size of the letters they are forming, to erase and replace them easily, and it provides an opportunity to practice the skill of holding a writing instrument. Simply copying the letters of the alphabet produces an eminently satisfying experience for very young children if they can use them to make their first words.

We know that it's difficult to carry a slate or clay letters or a sand tray to show parents and friends, so these activities lead the youngsters to pencil and paper where they continue to practice writing. We use unlined, 8½-by-11-inch paper cut in half and large-diameter, 3½-inch-long, super-soft, round lead pencils without erasers. As we said earlier, the traditional one-inch lined paper with the dotted line halfway between the solid lines confines writing to a prescribed space and imposes restrictive sizes on minds and hands that aren't ready to be confined. Such restrictions actually shift the focus of a child's thinking from what they want to write to how to write a letter at a time.

Paper and pencil produce solid evidence of effort and learning that is completely portable and doesn't rub off. It's a symbol to children of their growing maturity. These first specimens can be carried in the hand, hung on the wall, taped on the refrigerator, or folded and stuffed in a pocket to be pulled out later and shown to parents and schoolmates.

Writing to Read gives children a paper record of their work in another form as well. The ten Work Journals with their programmed words and their new words serve this purpose.

As an additional piece of evidence, at the end of each Work Journal there is a place for the teacher to sign and comment. The child is then given the journal to take home with the idea that he will write the same words for his parents. This is a prideful thing. It says, "I'm going to show that I can write cat, dog, and fish."

This act enlists the parent to confirm and add affirmative support to the child's work. Here research tells us that parental encouragement is vital if children are to learn well in school.

In addition to these other opportunities to produce hard copy, the ultimate piece for the child is produced at the typewriter. From the very first session in the Writing to Read center children are given basic instructions on how to use the typewriter, and that very day, after working on the computer, they use the typewriter to practice their first words. Of course, they also continue to practice and to experiment with pencil and paper and with slate and chalk.

The children in Writing to Read use the typewriter every day to hunt and peck the words they have learned from the computer. As the new words accumulate, they tend initially to type lists of those words. As they learn to make new words, these will appear in those lists as a prelude to the next step. They then begin to write their first sentences. The typewriter, for reasons we scarcely understand, becomes a powerful instrument to give them much satisfaction. By this time they are also able to read what they have typed.

We don't really know why typewriting is such a special and satisfying piece of technology to children. You can see its magic when you watch the faces of children as they work. For fifty years, the typewriter has been known to have important and positive effects on children's learning, but the many research studies that have repeated and reconfirmed the original and definitive findings of Professor Ben Wood have been largely ignored. In his classic study, published in 1932, a study that involved more than 5,000 children in the elementary grades, Wood discovered conclusive evidence that daily exposure to a typewriter improved a child's learning in every academic subject, including reading, writing, and arithmetic.

The very first time a child sits at the typewriter he or she may type *cat* five or six times. This is a considerable achievement because it shows them that they actually know what they are doing. After typing single words several times during these early days, the next thing the child will do is type a list of six or eight different words. (We don't encourage the copying of sentences from the blackboard because this can be a deceptive act. It fools us into thinking that a child really knows what it is he is copying.)

Then one day, in the midst of a list a new word will appear that can't be found anywhere in the previous work. Such a word—"mynace" for example—may not be recognizable by an adult but to the child it's *mayonnaise*. Or it may be a more recognizable word like *sink* but spelled "sinc," or *black* spelled "blac" or "blak." These are important milestones in a child's growing understanding of how words can be made as well as heard.

The typewriter, preferably with a golf-ball or daisywheel typing element (as opposed to older models with flying keys, which jam and frustrate children), is the perfect instrument for a child to use.

The typewriter adds to children's learning because:

1. Selecting and typing a letter on the keyboard is much easier than creating letters by hand
2. Typed letters are always perfect
3. Electric typewriters respond easily to the pressure of children's fingers
4. Letters are typed left to right, which reinforces directionality
5. It is beneficial for hand-eye coordination
6. Mastering the typewriter helps the development of writing skills
7. Typing is fun.

If you have a typewriter at home, make it available to your child as soon as there is an interest in writing. If you have a home computer and a printer, it will provide the same kind of hard copy as a typewriter with just a little additional keyboard work. We've found, however, that when it comes to typing, children don't respond quite as well to the display terminal of a computer as they do to a piece of paper in the typewriter. If you don't have a printer with your computer, then even the best efforts of the child are lost because seeing something on the screen is just not as good as holding it in the hand. If you recall when you last brought a present to your very young child, the child would jump all over you to get his or her hands on the package. This wasn't because the child was greedy or even that curious about the contents, only that the present in *your* hand simply wasn't real. The child had to have it in *his* or *her* hands to have the hard evidence that it really existed. The same is true of writing on a computer screen. The creative process is there, but the product is not real if, like television, the picture fades when the power is turned off. The hard evidence, like the present, is in someone else's hands. The computer printer may be a substitute for the immediacy of the product made on a typewriter, but as yet, we don't know.

## MASTERY

To know something, and to know it without the anxiety of doubt, is a wonderful feeling. That is mastery.

The grading system used in the world of education, in which a passing grade is a percentage of the whole, can be justified by the fact that no one knows everything there is to know. But the fact is, we seldom know with certainty those things we think we do know. We are a population that has been educated to believe that knowing 75 percent of something is good enough to get by and knowing 60 percent of something is often sufficient.

Knowing this, in the development of Writing to Read we defined for ourselves the task of devising an approach that would make it possible for a child to know something and know it well enough to be able to say, "I know how to do that." Early in our research, under the influence of Benjamin Bloom, who lifted the concept of mastery to a learning principle, I observed a group of children hard at work clearly understanding what they were doing. I wrote, "The children knew, and they knew that they knew." To me, and to them, that's not 90 percent, that's 100 percent, and that's an empowering thing. We believe that it is possible to stimulate the brain to produce that mental sureness and inner sense of competency when children learn how to complete a task and know that they have learned how.

This sense of pride that comes from knowing that you know is built into the Writing to Read program. The idea that a learner can and will learn everything set forth in a series of lessons is often taken for granted, as are the other basic ingredients of a learning situation—a self-motivated learner, adequate resources for the job, and a supporting relationship between teacher and student. Unfortunately, this combination exists too seldom, and thus the results of education are limited. The wide variation in results is a combination of many things, including overlarge and impersonal schools charged with the job of teaching large numbers of children, a constantly shifting and diverse school population, inadequate teacher training, textbooks poorly written, and classrooms of thirty to forty children that overpower even dedicated teachers. Under these conditions mastery can become a vague abstraction.

Bloom felt children are able to learn regardless of differences in their mental abilities if the children who learn more slowly are given the necessary time to learn. Implicit in this hypothesis is that the material to be learned needs to be organized so that you actually know when you know something. If the material is disorganized, perceptions of learning will be vague. If goals are also vague, results will be too. There has to be a beginning, a middle, and an end, and some precision in that arrangement. This doesn't mean the things to be learned have to be reduced to simplistic fragments, but that there needs to be a clear explanation of the task. This is true whether it's arithmetic or geography or writing or reading or learning to use the computer—and it's true whether you're a child or an adult.

So, in the Writing to Read System, when a child finishes word exercises on the computer, a Mastery Test is presented. The computer asks that the words in that cycle be typed—*cat,* for example, which is asked in the very first cycle. A built-in timer allows a reasonable period of several seconds for the completion of that typing. If a child exceeds that time or makes two errors in trying to type the word, the program loops back to the beginning of the lesson on the word. At that point the child may recognize his error or go on with that word exercise. At any step he can stop and hit the escape key that loops the program back into the Mastery Test. If the error is repeated, the program once more loops back to the exercises in the *cat* sequence until mastery occurs on the test. In later cycles, as the child learns the phonemes and the words that contain them, he can move directly to the Mastery Test. If he makes errors in the test, the program loops back and he gets to continue the lesson in more detail, or up to the point where he wants to try the test again. The machine accommodates its responses to the level of each child, contributing to children's ability to know what they are doing.

What is the final result? We think it is knowing and knowing that you know. That's mastery.

Again, a word of caution. Self-direction, hard copy, and mastery are important increments of learning theory that add to the strength of the Writing to Read program whether it is being taught with the use of a computer or at home. Neglect any of these elements and the system will be weakened and some children will learn less. Writing to Read is a system in which all the parts are important.

# CHAPTER 8

# CHILD DEVELOPMENT AND LEARNING

Sometimes some mothers wear an apron to clean up the house. Sum mothers wear aprons to cook super. My Mother dos not wear an apron. She dos no hav an apron. She wears a tshert and sum old blue jens to clean up the house. She wears the same thing whin she cooks super. I wish she wood wear an apron. I think she wood look vere prite. she looks prite even without an apron. But I wish she wood wear it. I do not think she would cook better if she wood wear an apron. She cooks vere good now.

Betty

BETTY WAS A first grader when she wrote this delightful little tribute to her mother. Certainly, she is a child who has internalized a healthy combination of reality and myth about her mother and mothers in general. It seems clear too that her mother cared for her, spent time with her, and attended to more than her basic needs.

This story is included here because the evidence is clear that parents who care for and pay attention to their children also raise children who learn better. We also know that pleasing parents is a powerful motivator for maturing children in every area of their development. Once they reach school, children also gain motivation by pleasing the teacher, which, though important, doesn't have the same long-term implications for a child. But in both cases, with parent and with teacher, the child gains when striving to please an adult.

There are many elements that contribute to a child's natural growth and development. Some of these elements, accidents of birth, are not within any parent's control, but many others are. In the course of observing thousands of children over the last four decades, I have determined that the most important contribution parents can make to the intellectual growth and the overall learning potential of their children at any age is a simple one. Parents merely have to do those things which in the normal course of life facilitate a child's growing language maturity. These are things that most parents provide as a natural part of child nurturing. They begin at birth and they continue throughout the growing years, if not throughout life. These things —which collectively can be called, in the simplest of terms, parental love—are shared equally by the mother and father. They include:

- General attention to the child and his or her physical and emotional needs from the moment of birth
- Word and noise play with the child at every opportunity, from the very first day
- The skin-to-skin touch of the hug, the nuzzle, the caress, and all the body vibrations that a child feels and hears when a parent is close
- Providing an overall presence that is comforting and reassuring.

Breast-feeding is one act that falls entirely to the mother, and it is the ultimate example of parental attention. Medical research has reconfirmed the wisdom of nature, finding breast-fed babies healthier, more disease resistant, and generally immune from colic. But physical health is only one part of the story. The skin touch of the mother's breast on the baby's cheek is a transmitter of much more than milk. This touch sends the message of security, warmth, and affection—qualities as necessary for the nutrition of a child's psyche as the mother's milk is for the nutrition of the child's body. And feeding time is usually a time for all those physical and verbal activities mentioned above. Of course, a child who is not breast-fed can be held with the same touch and maternal affection, but breast-feeding provides an added dimension and greater depth to that feeling, according to child development studies.

So from birth, the role of the mother and, to a slightly lesser extent, the father is that of a supportive communicator of affection, of language, and of the world. Most parents provide this kind of affection and care, but in some homes it isn't available to the child for a variety of reasons. The children from those homes arrive at school with much less inclination to learn and to please, and quite possibly less ability to learn as well.

The combination of this parental care and chronological maturity soon leads to the development of the child's first words, somewhere between the ninth and the fifteenth month, the range of thoroughly normal development. It should not surprise anyone that those first words are more often than not "Mama" and "Dada." But soon other common words surface and then sometimes strange words for a brother or sister. Brother Robert may be called "BB" and sister Doris "Sasa." There is no real reason for this, it's simply a combination of a child's perception of that person or thing and normal vocalization practices, both of which are skills which are being learned and not under control at all times. But these words will be directed at a particular person or thing and they will be consistent. Pets receive the same treatment. In our family, our son called a German shepherd named Skipper by the name "Hawhee," as if he were some form of mule.

By about three years of age, children are speaking in sentences and they have a developing vocabulary that expands daily if they are in an atmosphere that invigorates and encourages their speech. At this point, when a child has begun to express complete thoughts, three elements become critical to full and well-rounded language development. These elements, the responsibility of the parents, continue to be important as a child matures and moves toward school age. The elements are talking, listening, and reading, and they all proceed in parallel, not one at a time.

## TALKING

When we speak of talking, we are referring to more than conversations between parents and the use of such commands with children as "Stop that," "Eat your lunch," and "Go to sleep." What we're suggesting is the establishment of an atmosphere in the home in which children are part of the picture, are talked to as little adults, are reasoned with, and are not told to be quiet. It is part of a general household ambiance that does not squelch anyone's speech. There was a time when it was thought that children were better seen than heard, and there are parts of our culture where it is the practice to tell children to be quiet, but what we mean isn't at all a question of simply tolerating or not tolerating noise. We're talking about the open invitation to speech and conversation that exists in some households and doesn't in others, the initiation of speech on the part of the parent and parental encouragement that leads the child to speak.

## LISTENING

What this open invitation to speech implies is the freedom of your child to talk at every opportunity, and it also implies parents listening, which is the second important element in the nurturing of language development in young children. Listening is not something that most people do well, therefore you may have to learn or relearn how to listen for the nuances and shades of meaning that quickly appear in a child's speech. It also means learning patience. Children constantly ask "Why?" to the point of annoyance. They say: "Why are stars?" "Why are airplanes?" "Why did you do that?" and on and on. It's important for parents to recognize that this "why" is as much an invitation to conversation as a request for information. This is the sort of invitation that should be responded to as close to the asking as possible, because a response is not only reassuring but it shows that you are interested in listening to what the child has to say.

## READING

The third element in the language development cycle is reading, and of course, as your child is unable to read, this means reading to your child. Children love stories of all kinds—from the simple to the complex, from the real to the fantastic. The local library is a source for children's books and a good source of information about them. Certainly there are good and poor stories, and some stories appeal to children more than others, but your child will be the best critic of your choices. As you read to your child you'll quickly recognize the phenomenon that out of the twenty-five or fifty books you will read to your child, one, possibly two, will be asked for every time you sit down to read. Long after you have become bored beyond tears, the child will continue to insist that that single story is the one he wants most of all. This actually serves a very useful purpose because you'll find after the eighth or ninth reading (or sooner) that the child has almost memorized the story and will follow the text with his finger. You'll soon learn, as well, that if you deviate from the text by a single word your child will correct you.

When is the best time to read together? No time is really best and any time is good, but after dinner or at bedtime is better, if both parents are to share in the reading.

The importance of reading to children can't be overstated because several things happen when a parent reads to a child:

- The child realizes that at that moment the two most important people in the world are participating—the child and the parent
- The closeness of the reading situation, the child sitting on the lap or close by in a chair or bed, engenders warmth, security, and affection
- It underscores the idea that there is pleasure to be derived from something in print
- As the process continues, the child responds by identifying the words with the meaning of those words.

"Reading to your children may be the single most powerful contribution that you, as a parent, can make toward their success in school," says Dr. William F. Russell, author of *Classics to Read Aloud to Your Children,* and I agree with him, but talking and listening are also terribly important preparatory activities for language development and language maturity in children. And the three elements combined create an excitement about speech and books while they carefully plant the idea that language and books are sources of pleasure.

## WRITING

When parents read to children, it also seems to reduce some of the irritants that exist in the beginning stages of learning to write and read, irritants that can easily add up to a lifelong disposition *not* to write and a concurrent lack of interest in reading. Unfortunately, these irritants are actually the basic mechanics of writing: spelling, grammar, syntax, punctuation, and sentence structure.

Fortunately, these mechanic's tools that are used to reach the goal of proper communication can be learned through hearing and use and need not be learned in these early years through drill. They are crucial to good writing, but as important as they are, they must remain subordinate functions in the process of learning to write.

The criteria for judging a piece of writing, whether created by an adult or a child, are what it says, and how clearly and how well it is said. How well it's spelled or punctuated is secondary. Today we have large numbers of college graduates who have been brought up on the proofreader mentality that emphasizes spelling, punctuation, and grammar at the expense of *learning* to write, and these people are unhappily convinced that they can't write. Of course, they can't, at least not without great effort and not well. This isn't to say that the rules of writing don't have historical validity or that they should be discarded, only that they have very little practical place in the first flush of learning.

Capital letters are a good example. Though we were schooled on the vital importance of capitalization, these uppercase letters are more decoration than anything else. They aren't identifiable at all in conversation, yet they are stressed in early learning far out of proportion to their importance.

Punctuation does add clarity. The presence or absence of commas, for example, is unquestionably important to the complete and perfect understanding of a text, but to make commas a fetish sets up another obstacle in learning to write that can destroy the entire process. *Destroy* isn't too strong a word here because absolute adherence to these rules can take all the joy, creativity, and spontaneity out of writing.

## PAIRED LEARNING

The one-on-one role is familiar to parents in the general context of working with their children on the first living skills—drinking from a glass, toilet training, shoe tying—but the role of parent as formal teacher, or even co-learner in an educational context, is usually a new one.

We know that when children work together in pairs learning is improved for both partners, and that in the end they make better and faster progress together than either would make alone. They help each other, and if the material is designed appropriately, they take turns and evenly distribute the opportunities for learning. Each child seems to profit from the two tasks involved—sometimes being tutored, sometimes acting as tutor. There is no paradox in alternating these roles, and this is a lesson that many adults can heed: People of comparatively equal ability can easily shift roles and help each other learn with no loss of self-esteem in the bargain.

Children also enjoy the sense of friendship ("I work with Joey over there") and the social support of a peer, which contrasts sharply to the awe or constraint which usually prevails when an adult is the only reviewer of the child's task. Getting immediate help from a peer when stuck brings great and instant relief, and the fear of failure is cushioned by the noncritical relationship between the two peers. This is healthy and educationally sound, but unfortunately, schools got twisted into thinking that helping is cheating. The impulses of giving and sharing are normal for most children.

The same positive premises cover parent and child pairing for learning. It may take a good deal of patience and restraint for a parent to sit through a fifteen- or twenty-minute session in which their child is trying to formulate sentences, but it's worth the effort for both and both will learn from it. Parents have to learn the difficult role of what I call being "flat-footed" with their children. This simply means getting away from the idea that children don't understand you and that to make them understand something you must talk down to them. Parents can talk to their children conversationally as they would other adults, that is, flat-footed. Sugar-coated entreaty, statements like "If you finish your soup now, we can go out for ice cream," are emotional bribery. And the little smiling faces drawn on the children's papers, so popular with teachers, are also bribery. Such tactics may produce fear and withdrawal in children because the child anticipates the censure that is sure to come later when there are errors. These corrections are verbalized in such phrases as "That's wrong" and "I don't understand why you can't do this the right way" and "You're never going to learn, are you?" Parents should avoid this kind of stern correction process because we know it has negative consequences. Correcting is not teaching, it is punishing. In the face of garbled efforts, parents and teachers should ask, "Tell me what it says. I can't understand it." Children will see for themselves and make their own corrections or they will ask for help.

## IMPEDIMENTS

We are a society deeply, and rightfully, concerned with the high number of adult and adolescent illiterates in this country, currently estimated at 27 million. Paradoxically we also have a high level of literacy. What is less well known is the fact that a substantial percentage of the American population can't write a decent paragraph, and this includes a great number of college graduates.

I feel this is largely due to the little irritants that combine to form major roadblocks along the path of learning. Our research with children has identified some of these abrasive factors in early learning, and though no single one of these factors is decisive, they accumulate like the water in a blister, become more and more painful, and finally discourage the act of learning itself. The feeling is somewhat akin to walking down the street with a small stone in your shoe. At first you notice a little irritation. As you continue to walk, the stone rubs the skin and it begins to hurt. If you keep walking, you eventually create a blister that interferes with walking entirely. Not learning to write is a process of accumulating a series of these minor irritants in the collective shoes of our literary brains.

Knowledge of these irritants underscores the fact that the very first writing experiences of a child are crucial and that care must be taken to remove these irritations.

The first little irritant occurs when kindergartners are given a seven-inch-long, hexagonal pencil with hard lead. Seven inches is too long; little fingers can't keep the pencil from waving all over the place. In an effort to keep the pencil under control, a child will hold it as tightly as possible right at the bevel point. This causes pain. Who doesn't remember those semipermanent indentations in the first and middle fingers of the writing hand? The hexagonal shape of pencils, a design which is only meant to keep pencils from rolling off the desk, contributes to the pain suffered from grasping too tightly.

Children also have a fear of puncturing paper with pencil points, and pencils with hard lead and sharp points grasped tightly in little hands quickly make holes in paper. The finger pain doesn't bother teachers but the holes in the paper certainly do, and teachers respond by admonishing a child not to press so hard. Of course, if you don't press hard, a hard lead pencil won't make any mark at all.

This combination of irritants is simple enough to avoid.

If pencils are round, cut in half (to about 3½ inches), and have supersoft lead (number one), all of the problems are solved and the writing instrument can be easily controlled without any tenacious squeezing. At the same time the soft lead flows smoothly leaving its mark for all to see.

The second major inhibitor of early writing is the universal assumption that children need to draw letters one inch high on paper that is prelined with an inch between lines and a dotted line dividing that inch. This immediately creates the idea in the child's mind that making a letter is like making a drawing. The whole process becomes an artistic presentation instead of a basic writing exercise. As adults, we're all familiar with the impatience we feel because the writing hand can't keep up with the brain. The typewriter helps us as adults, and the word processor helps even more, but we continue to force children into an artificial, molasses-slow speed so that they must laboriously draw a letter at a time. They move so slowly and mechanically, with artistic considerations taking primacy over the function of writing, that they often forget what they are writing before they finish it. Then, this error is brought into clear focus when, after spending so much time in kindergarten and first grade on the aesthetics of drawing letters, along comes cursive writing and all those carefully taught aesthetics of calligraphy and hours and hours of penmanship drills go right out the classroom window.

In the same category as the aesthetic beauty of each written letter is the idea that a child's writing must be neat and clean. This is often done in schools so that the child's work can be proudly displayed on parents' night. Unfortunately, the assumption that writing, especially first drafts, must be neat is more than a pebble in the shoe, it is a boulder. All writing is the process of rewriting, and from the first day a child should be taught that writing is a messy process, that things usually are not done right the first time, that things go wrong, that ideas change, and that therefore neatness is secondary to content and intent.

If all of these impediments to writing can be removed, children will be off and winging. If only some of them can be removed, progress will still occur but it may be slower.

All of this is to say: Make things as easy as possible, listen to your child, talk to your child, read to your child, work with your child, and above all be patient and sensitive to the needless irritations of the materials your child uses. Chalk and slate are among the oldest forms of writing tools and remain among the best.

# CHAPTER 9

# TWO IMPORTANT TOOLS: THE COMPUTER AND THE TYPEWRITER

In kindergardin I love going to the chalenj corse. I love working. I love the cumpooter room. I love the riting sinter. I līk the computer room bēcos we go to the computers and the typewriters to and the gām and the book sinter. Thin we rēd a storē. Thin we tāc a nap and when we wāc up we ēt a snac. Next we go out sīd and then cum in to hav shō and tel. Tin we will rēd a short storē.

## THE COMPUTER

I BEGAN THE work of putting the Writing to Read design into a computer program in order to take advantage of the speed, versatility, and patience of the computer as a delivery system. I had decided that it was best to get as automated as the technology would permit. In the wonderful world of computer technology, the so-called "state of the art" changes so rapidly that it has been necessary to use the most sophisticated learning theories to construct a software program to match the capabilities of the equipment. Unfortunately, this has seldom been done.

I was drawn to the computer because it has a number of obvious advantages as a teaching tool—speed of operation, memory capacity, and flexibility—and some not so obvious advantages, like the opportunity it offers to limit the errors that can be made in the presentation of material.

It can help teachers serve the greatest number of children by making maximum use of their time. I wasn't looking for something "teacher proof," because the role of the adult, of the teacher in the classroom, is critically important to the success of any educational system. I didn't envision a sterile room where children are taught in isolation, surrounded by whirring technology.

What I did see was the shift away from methods of teaching centered on and solely dependent upon the quality of a teacher. Teaching remains an excessively labor-intensive activity. There is nothing inherently wrong in a school where the only technology is the teacher, a book, a piece of chalk, and a blackboard; but large classes, transient student populations, insufficient operating budgets, and erratic use of technology limit teachers' effectiveness.

On the other hand, I was also keenly aware that the computer industry and some educators were making outrageous predictions about the future of computers and education. There was talk of the awesome power of the computer and the ability of the high-tech revolution to create massive changes in education. In the face of these blustery arguments I tried to keep in mind what John Dewey said many years ago: "Beware of the argument that proves too much." The industry was talking too much and too loudly, and it seemed clear to me that despite what was being said, the computer was not going to be a panacea.

Thomas Alva Edison wrote before 1900 that his invention of the motion picture projector would make books obsolete in the schools. Children would no longer have to read books, prognosticators said, because everything would be brought to them on the screen in greater attractiveness and detail than any print media could match, even with the generous use of illustrations. The same was said of radio. In the early 1920s, General Sarnoff and others in the industry predicted that the radio would produce a revolution in education. Similar predictions were made for television in the early 1950s, and anyone who has been to school in the last thirty-five years knows that none of these technologies was ever used to its potential.

Now, history was repeating itself in the mid-1970s. Article after article appeared overstating the case for computers and claiming that they would "absolutely be the final word in . . . ," "finally result in . . . ," "bring about the long awaited . . ." educational changes that movies, radio, and TV were never able to accomplish.

We should keep in mind, however, that it might not be the technology that has historically been at fault but the educational establishment that has failed to accept it. In fact, all that the recital of the failures of earlier technology proves to me is that the schools are relatively impenetrable when it comes to adopting powerful technologies.

In more than forty years of experience I've found that schools can mimic oysters, a form of life that ingests large quantities of seawater, filters it, and retains the necessary nutrients for life. The filter process removes almost all the impurities, but occasionally a grain of sand remains and becomes an irritant. The oyster uses an ingenious way of handling this nonejectable material; it pearls it over. This is what the educational system has done to technology over the years. Motion pictures, radio, and television are all in the schools, but their peripheral use, their subordinate and supplemental roles have, in effect, pearled them over. They are neither irritants nor particularly effective.

The typewriter is a good case in point. Even this most common of labor-saving devices has been shunted aside as too advanced or too expensive for general classroom use. The meticulous research on the educational uses of the typewriter conducted by Dr. Ben Wood was greeted with widespread apathy. Wood talked of the general power of technology in education as far back as 1929 when Macmillan published his book, *The Motion Picture in the Classroom*. In it, he said the technology of the motion picture was "a powerful learning device capable of extraordinary use in enhancing children's learning." Little happened. In 1932, under the sponsorship of the Carnegie Foundation for the Advancement of Learning, Dr. Wood published a study of the effect of the typewriter on the academic skills of some 5,000 children. Children using typewriters, he found, gained more in every academic area than the children in the control populations.

I decided to use the computer because it is a combination of all the audiovisual devices invented in the last 100 years. It combines elements of the typewriter, the movie projector, the radio, a television set, an overhead projector, and a tape recorder, and it becomes more than the sum of all of these parts because, unlike the others, it will react to the user with considerably more than a mere letter when a key is pressed. The term that describes this reaction is "interactive," because a properly programmed computer will change its response in reaction to the user's behavior.

The Writing to Read System has been designed with sophisticated software that allows enough flexibility so that one child's response will cause the computer to react differently than another child's. In playing the Cat and Mouse game, the speed with which a child reacts is recorded by the computer's memory and that initial speed modifies the speed at which the computer reacts on the next attempt by the child to complete a given exercise.

Follow this example. The screen shows a very short story:

A fat cat, with a hat, wants to catch a mouse in his house.

In this case, the idea is to have the child type *mouse*. The speed with which a child types *mouse* is monitored by the computer, and it adjusts itself to respond to that child's typing speed. If the child types fast enough, the mouse makes its way safely to the mouse hole. If the word is typed too slowly or mistakes are made, the cat puts his hat on top of the mouse. The faster the child types *mouse*, the faster the cat moves. These are the computer properties that make it interactive. What the child does changes what the computer does.

In the winter of 1979–80 I began to test computer designs and programs with kindergarten children selected at random from the general population of a small town on the east coast of Florida. The results of these studies were sent to a number of professional colleagues, including Dr. William Turnbull, then president of the Educational Testing

Service in Princeton, New Jersey, and Dr. Alvin C. Eurich, president of the Academy of Educational Development, Inc., in New York City. After reviewing the findings with Dr. Eurich, Dr. Turnbull called to tell me that he thought the research data on the results of the Writing to Read System made a significant contribution to early childhood educa- tion. He and Dr. Eurich thought the concept should be dem- onstrated for a larger audience of computer manufacturers and software publishers at a meeting they would sponsor. I agreed, a meeting was scheduled for December 15, 1980, and the executives of most of the major computer firms and publishers met at the ETS Conference Center in Princeton. We arranged to have twelve children brought from the non- reading kindergarten and first grade classes in Trenton, New Jersey, public schools to demonstrate the effects of the program. Following a morning discussion by the partici- pants on the then very limited use of computers by the schools across the country, we demonstrated the Writing to Read computer program.

Two computers were set up in the large conference cen- ter lobby, a huge two-story room with a vaulted ceiling and a massive stone fireplace. Two pairs of youngsters, accom- panied by their kindergarten teachers, walked into this in- timidating setting and sat down at the computers as they had for fifteen-minute sessions on each of the two preceding days. One of the children was being tutored in typing the word *dog*. The computer asked the child to type *dog*. Having successfully typed the letter *d*, the child kept hitting the *a* key instead of the *o* key. The machine prompted the child to type the sound "o," as it's programmed to do, and then waited for the right response. Two tries, three, five, nine, fourteen tries, and everyone in the room, including the child's partner, was overcome with anxiety.

I had advised the teacher who had accompanied the children not to hover around and not to prompt the children—but here was this poor child making fifteen errors in a row, and I said to myself, Why doesn't she do something to help this poor boy? Before the demonstration the two children had been told that they could help each other, but now the second child had withdrawn and was of no help.

The frustrated boy kept plugging away and finally lifted his face to the high, dark ceiling and said defiantly, "There's something wrong here." At least that broke the tension. I was about to violate my own rules when the child jerked erect and triumphantly struck the *o* key. There was an audible sigh of relief from our skeptical audience.

The point of this story is that in the classroom this waiting for the right response, this tolerance of error, is impossible. If a question is asked and there is a wrong answer or a child wants to think for a second, the class cannot wait. If you take a slow count of one to ten to allow a child to grope for an answer, that's considerably longer than is psychologically acceptable in the mind of the teacher and the children. And it's that groping, that effort to be rational, that is of critical importance. Such thinking results in learning. At the same time it is that lack of meditative calm that is a serious deficiency in mass instruction, and it results in many missed learning opportunities. Such use of the computer can add greatly to children's learning.

In the final analysis, the demonstration in Princeton showed dramatically that children from urban schools could be taught to type words after less than forty-five minutes of exposure to Writing to Read. A nationally known educator present at this session said to the group later: "I have been watching children for a long time and I don't recall any single situation in which a teacher would have had the patience or the inclination to wait that long for a child to find the right response. I think I've seen something extremely rare here."

As further evidence of the influence of the computer on education, it's necessary to note only the fact that before 1980 there was scarcely a university with a computer science department in its school of education. Today there is scarcely a school without such a department and there are several national and international organizations that meet regularly to consider the future of computers in education.

Remarkably, there is very little good educational software available, despite the fact that virtually every major publisher has moved into (and some have moved out of) the computer software field in education. Thus far, computer-assisted instruction has been dominated by the question and answer, multiple choice, true-false state of mind. This is a limited use of the technology, but perhaps it can be justified on the grounds that some studies show that even such limited and supplementary use of the computer enhances learning and that children taught with computers tend to score higher than those who have no computers. The computer seems to be such a powerful energizer that even when it is poorly fed with software, it still delivers.

And surprisingly, the software designers have failed to recognize the importance of the human voice as a vital communications tool in learning. Since learning is never easy, it's hard to understand this lack. In the absence of such programming, the schools have bought huge supplies of software with no voice capability, the equivalent of hiring teachers who are not able to speak.

Discussions of the impact of all technology on teaching and learning proceed from some assumptions drawn from the Industrial Revolution, namely that new technology will make it possible to do those things that were previously done by hand, more quickly, more efficiently, hence more cheaply. Applied to education, such thinking frightens people who are concerned with children's healthy growth. Many say, and I agree, that children are not cotton to be woven more efficiently with a power loom. Psychologists, parents, and teachers are worried that computerizing learning, particularly for the very young, may dehumanize a process that needs to be full of warmth and adult encouragement. It's true, after all, that although a computer can reduce the level of a child's frustration, it can't apply a bandage to a skinned elbow or hug away a frightening experience, but it can and does deliver individualized, continuous attention to the learner.

The critics of computer teaching are making statements that are as farfetched as those who claim the computer is a cure-all, statements that are just not consistent with facts. It is being said that education by computer will cause children to become psychopathic and that it will stifle their imaginations since computers, like psychopaths, do everything effortlessly and without inhibition. This, they say, is education without soul. This lack of soul, I suppose, means lack of contact with the reality of pencil, paper, teacher, and so forth. There is another false argument that claims that pushing children into using the computer somehow deprives them of their childhood. In my experience, the computer has never replaced normal childish play, and since the decline in the popularity of the frenetic computer games of the "shoot 'em down in space" genre, the concern that electronic-game playing will keep children from other kinds of play has also diminished.

What happens is quite the opposite. The computer, by reducing the amount of failure in the earliest days of school, removes the lifetime trauma of feeling mentally inadequate, the largest unnoted cause of dropouts, later violence, unemployment, and crime. The word-processing capability of the computer allows a child to focus on writing and the ways to improve it without having to worry about the troublesome problem of handcrafting the letters of the words that he is thinking.

Beyond being faster and cheaper, however, many educators feel there is nothing fundamentally different educationally in computer technology except the delivery system itself. In fact, computers aren't very accomplished at some things. A human teacher is an excellent and discriminating hearer of sounds and words a child speaks, and can identify good pronunciation and intonation at a distance even when the whole class is talking at once.

Often, however, new technology permits entirely different things to happen. A teacher has difficulty in quickly responding to the qualities of the writing of a group of students or even a single student without some form of assistance. This is something the computer can do very well. From elementary school to college, the development of writing skills is a painful trial for many on both sides of the teacher's desk. It is now possible for computers to enter the scene, offer critical help, and affect the final product. The computer is clearly not restricted by wearying drill and repetition, and thus we now can begin to plan computer curricula in which elements of syntax and grammar are taught, rules for the correct placement and use of clauses and sentences are introduced, and semantic checks made against equivalency word lists like those in a thesaurus. Other variations on this process can check the agreement of person, number, and tense and prompt the writer to vary sentence structure and variety when necessary.

A very simple example of this, now being developed for use in conjunction with Writing to Read, is a beginning dictionary that can be used to identify words either by conventional spelling or phonemic spelling. If a word is entered in the phonemic format, a pointer takes the searcher to the conventional spelling, where the full definition of the word is found, as well as the phonemic spelling.

I have never been worried by the fact that part of the appeal of a device such as the typewriter or a computer is that it obviates the need to master a difficult skill like handwriting as a precondition for written communication. We'll continue to teach children how to write with pencil and paper. When voice-recognition devices become part of the computer, we will want to teach the use of that medium to the young as well, and we'll want to continue to teach handwriting, typewriting, and computing too.

The point of such examples isn't to dwell on the marvels of the recent past and those on the horizon, but to suggest that there is a natural fit between the nature of the skills of the educator and the parent, and the role of appropriate technology. The very speed which makes the keyboard a matter of convenience for skilled adults also makes it a teaching tool for those learning to write.

In Writing to Read there are no consequences attached to an incorrect response and no praise for correct ones. There are no rebuffs, no pleasing bells or chafing whistles or visual admonishments on the screen, and there is no cheering either. Errors just do not work. The screen does say simply, "Try again," and this is sufficient to encourage further learning. A correct answer causes the program to move to the next step. What we've tried to do is remove both the whipped cream and the vinegar from the task of learning.

The ability of the computer to count, time, and repeat allows us to structure lessons that give directions, define and record progress, require success as a condition of progress to the next episode, and move the child through the structure systematically, patiently, and at an individualized pace. This is what interaction is all about. As much as possible, Writing to Read utilizes the reinforcers of mastering the material and of the practical payoff of being able to communicate by means of the written word.

To compose for this instrument that is a combination of a television screen, the audio of radio, and the keyboard of a typewriter, all linked by logic and memory, and to make it intelligent enough to meet the true needs of the learner is a challenge. To meet these needs we combined visual presentations of words and graphics that depict those words, and then put the graphics in motion. Graphics are powerful entry points into the human mind and an aid to the understanding of complex concepts.

A visual representation can frequently clarify meaning, and the computer makes possible an additional graphic dimension because it can simulate motion. To represent the fact that a word on the computer screen is an assemblage of symbols, letters, each of which carries a sound, the word first appears with the graphic drawing of that word—a turtle or a house or a cat. Movements of the letters show how the word is constructed as the letters move to and from the edges of the screen. The graphic movement says to the child that the word *cat* is an assembly of three symbols that represent the sounds in the word *cat*. This principle is followed for each of the thirty words that comprise the core of the Writing to Read program.

We talked earlier about the senses of sight, hearing, taste, smell, and touch forming pipelines to the brain. To remove any of those lines to the brain is possibly to deny (by accident or neglect) the single most powerful means by which a particular child takes in information. As we've said, in some children hearing may not be as important as seeing, and in others it is the reverse. Since all normal people use at least those two senses to complement and reinforce each other the removal of either denies the brain information or reinforcement, or the ability to comprehend that particular information at all.

We've included the audio element in Writing to Read

because all learning is helped by the human voice and because it is integral to the nature of the subject to be learned here—reading and writing. We're teaching children that the sounds they speak can be made visible so it's important that the computer speak those sounds. A child may see and hear the letter *a*. A picture may evoke the name of a letter but not the sound in the word *cat*. A silent computer can't do this. If the talking computer isn't available the same job can be done verbally by a parent with a recorded tape, but it is essential that the sounds be verbalized to and by a child.

On the computer screen we show a picture of a cat, the computer says the word "cat" and then the word *cat* appears on the screen. It's critical that the child begin to understand all three sides of this triangle of three symbols—picture, voice, and word—all abstract symbols of a real cat. The three sides are introduced to a child's brain so that they may become mental synonyms for each other. We move from one level of abstract symbolism to another, from the picture to the spoken word to the word, and they help meld, like a series of overlays, the idea of the word's identity in the child's brain. Such subliminal learning, the subtle absorption of a concept without conscious awareness, is at the root of much learning and is also the basis of much research in artificial intelligence.

## THE TYPEWRITER

The Writing to Read software program is not currently available for home use, so the special qualities of the computer aren't presently available to you as a parent. Don't be discouraged; Writing to Read will be available and hopefully soon. However, the electric typewriter is an effective parallel piece of technology that can be used now. We used the typewriter in the early development of Writing to Read and we were able to accomplish a great deal. At this point, then, let's take a closer look at the important elements of the typewriter.

The typewriter's main advantages are that it produces a perfect letter each time a key is struck and that it responds quickly enough so that the typist doesn't have to stop thinking about the letters that are going to be written in order to reproduce those words, as is often necessary in writing longhand. For a child this is especially important, because the interval between action (striking a key) and reinforcement (a letter on the page) is drastically shortened. For children, the arduous work of shaping letters is removed from the writing process, and the speed of the machine is much closer to a child's thought processes.

The voluminous research in this area has shown that the typewriter appeals to young children for other reasons as well. First, the typewriter makes one child's writing as good as the next's. There is no need to compare penmanship. The child who normally makes a mess of written work becomes as neat and pristine as his friends when he uses a typewriter. Second, children quickly realize that they are writers, that they are "on paper," and they can easily show the results of their work to other people. And third, the act of typing requires very little effort even for tiny fingers. There is no pencil to hold and no way to poke a hole in the paper. This relieves a good deal of the unseen pressure involved in learning to write through penmanship drills.

Despite its ease of operation, however, the typewriter presents problems for children because it is poorly designed for adults:

- The platen, the surface against which the typewriter keys strike, is below the level of the typist's eyes. Seeing what you have typed requires lifting yourself up to look down into the machine. Put two-by-four-inch planks under the rear feet of the machine for better viewing.
- It's a bother to have to roll up the platen each time you want to check what you've typed just because you don't sit high enough in your chair to be able to see into the machine.
- On the other hand, the widespread idea that a five-year-old's fingers are too small to cover the

keyboard is incorrect. They can reach all the keys without strain.

The common arrangement, called the Qwerty keyboard, was designed for typewriters with keys that swing up to hit the ribbon. For that reason it was necessary to separate the most used keys so that when two keys were struck simultaneously they wouldn't jam at the platen. Not only that, but the *a* and the *e,* the most-used keys, are in difficult locations for children and require the use of the weakest and hardest-to-control fingers. The Dvorak keyboard, named after its designer, relocates the keys so that the first fingers on both hands do the majority of the work. Unfortunately, even though research has shown that all typists, new and retrained, gain remarkably in speed and accuracy with the Dvorak keyboard, it is difficult to overcome 100 years of inertia.

One other problem, from a teaching point of view, is that all the keys of the typewriter are labeled in capital (uppercase) letters. Since no less than 90 percent of all typing is done in lowercase letters, this identification makes absolutely no sense and is confusing to children who wonder which form is correct. A parent can correct this problem by relabeling the keys with homemade paste-ons.

Remember to place the typewriter no higher than twenty-four inches from the floor, and make sure your child can sit with both feet on the floor.

These problems, however, are minor compared to the value of the typewriter in stimulating children. Observers have remarked for more than fifty years on this neglected adjunct to learning. My own speculations on why the instrument is dynamic in its appeal to children lies in its capacity to give children "hard copy." They like to have something in their hands, real evidence of their work.

# CHAPTER 10

# THE SYMBOLIC TRIANGLE: SPEAKING, HEARING, SEEING

CHILDREN SPEAK ALMOST as unconsciously as they breathe, so it's important for parents to recognize and understand that many times their child isn't speaking discreet words, but whole concepts. Children run words together in a flow of sounds. They say, "donwana," "aingona," and "somi." We, too, speak in an uninterrupted flow, pausing for emphasis or clarity. Children understand what they are saying perfectly and we usually do, too, but we have to help them recognize that the flow of sounds that makes up "donwana" or "do not want to" is really made up of several small parts called

w . . . o . . . r . . . d . . . s.

Children must be helped to hear and then visualize single words and to understand that when that single word can be seen, it is a physical representation of the word that was spoken. In the beginning it was a word that was made up of a sound or series of sounds. Therefore, what we want to try to do is to have the child consciously begin to "see" that there are three levels of symbolization:

1. A spoken word or series of sounds which represents something, like "bread"
2. A two-dimensional drawing of a loaf of bread, which is an abstract, visual symbol equal to the oral symbol

**3.** A written word-symbol that stands for both the picture of bread and the sounds of the spoken word.

These principles are the three elements that make it possible for children to learn to write and read. So the use of the visual word *b-r-e-a-d* is the ultimate abstraction for the reality. At the two preceding symbolic levels—first a spoken word and then a drawing of the object named by the word—a child has some early competency. So we move the child to the point where he sees that a word made visible on a piece of paper is a series of letters and that those letters stand as symbols of the sounds made when the word is spoken. This is a considerable intellectual achievement and certainly not one that children are able to verbalize. They can, however, understand it without too much difficulty. To facilitate the process we move through exercises in which the sound, the picture, and the word are gradually melded into a single idea.

To do this we appeal to the variety of sensory aptitudes children exhibit and we use a variety of sensory materials as we explained in chapter 6. There are things to be seen, felt, and heard, and since we don't know which child learns best from which set of sensory stimuli, we set up a cafeteria of materials, all of which have the same object in mind—the learning of the sounds in words and the concept of the alphabet. From a finger in the sand and a pencil on paper to thin clay strings and letters cut from emery cloth, the children initially are encouraged to try them all.

There are two ways parents can help ensure the conceptualization of this idea by their children. We have already talked about both of them but they are so important that they are worth emphasizing again.

## TALKING

There has been a great deal of research on the size and depth of the average child's vocabulary when he or she enters kindergarten at four or five years of age. Twenty years ago, the evidence indicated a vocabulary of nearly 5,000 words, but the research on which that figure was based was gathered largely from suburban school districts across the country and did not reflect the size or nature of the vocabulary of urban children.

The most up-to-date research shows that the average child begins school with an oral vocabulary of between 2,300 and 2,700 words. In-depth studies of children's syntax, that is, the grammatical complexity of their speech, indicates that they use nearly all the sophisticated forms of sentence structure used by adults. Children speak in compound and complex sentences, and they use *and* and *because* as connectors to accomplish this. Unfortunately, the schools use primary reading texts that don't take this level of sophistication into account.

We knew from the outset that Writing to Read was having little or no effect on some children and we wanted to try to find out why. Our efforts to examine the nature of the vocabulary of those children uncovered the fact that they were nearly all noncommunicative children with seriously limited vocabularies, often less than 200 words. Without exception, their vocabularies consisted of only the basics—such words as *stove, floor, eat, run, jump, cry,* and *mad*. They usually talked with their bodies, making faces, hand gestures, and shoulder and head movements, as much as with their mouths. Our program quite simply did not have the capacity to overcome the severe language deficits of these children, though Writing to Read did penetrate into children with limited vocabularies to a greater extent than we anticipated. Our initial research population of more than 900 children produced less than 30 for whom our program was ineffective.

Our extrapolation from this research was that a good speaking vocabulary, learned at home, was essential to the initial writing and reading process. This finding, though at first shocking, brought to mind an exchange I had in the 1950s with Abba Eban, who had been Israel's minister of education. I was invited to a reception for Eban by the hostess because she thought he would enjoy talking to an American educator. After some casual conversation, he and I withdrew to a private room and began talking about the state of education in our two countries. This was approximately the period when Americans were discovering, belatedly, the inadequacy of our system of education for urban children, especially children of the poor and children of the poor who were black. Eban was aware of our problem and spoke to me about some of Israel's findings which he felt might be relevant to our situation.

They had determined, he said, that the children of the immigrants that were returning to Israel in large numbers from Arab states were having great difficulty in the Israeli schools in competition with the children of European immigrants. The research showed that the largest single element in this disparity was the limited vocabulary of the children of illiterate parents who themselves often had an oral vocabulary of 800 words or less. The Israelis felt that vocabulary and simple language deficiencies were the root causes of the difficulty of these children learning in school and in learning to read and write in particular.

This conversation and the similarity of the Israeli findings served as background for my thinking in the development of Writing to Read twenty years later, because we were employing a system that used children's speech as its basis. Thus, I was conscious of the fact that children with serious deficits in the maturational level of their speech would come to Writing to Read with a handicap that the program might overcome, or conversely, which might by its very nature be the root cause of the program's ineffectiveness.

This is all to say that by encouraging children's speech, by enhancing it and responding to it, by having exercises that encourage speech, by having them "show and tell" with frequency, with an invitation to verbal complexity and sophistication, we avoid these early problems that are based on insufficient opportunities to learn to speak. In Writing to Read the child's speech is at the very root of the child learning to read and write.

This said, let it be noted that we tend to neglect the importance of speech for children, both in its contribution to their mental maturation and in its relationship to learning to read and write. Under typical school conditions learning to read seems to be remote from children's speaking. Word-frequency lists are used as arbiters of what is appropriate for children's textbooks. These lists are based on the frequency with which words appear in books. And many of these studies include counts of the word-frequency vocabulary of the front page of the *New York Times*. The words most common in the spoken vocabulary of children should be the basis for their reading books with an occasional word that stretches their minds and their experiences.

The primers and first grade texts used today contain, in general, a vocabulary of about 400 words, and that is twice as high as it was forty years ago. The feeling has been that children have less trouble reading one-syllable words and simple sentences. Yet children find no more difficulty in recognizing *airplane* than the word *that*, and in fact, *that* may be the more difficult of the two.

To develop children's speech, then, they must live in an atmosphere where speech is heard and where their own speech is listened to. The house may be filled with the sound of words in the form of the noise of television, radio, or records, but this is actually noise which suppresses speech, not words that add to vocabulary. Television, for example, might be helpful if children watched attentively, but they don't. The "Children's Television Workshop" is an obvious exception to this, but it has the problem of being of least interest in those homes where it is needed most.

The role of the adult, of the parent, is crucial here. Children need to be invited to talk and they should be encouraged to make up their own stories. Until the age of five children live comfortably between reality and fantasy. A dragon or unicorn is as real to a child as an elephant or a camel, and it's possible that none of them have ever been seen by the child. On the other hand, children will manufacture fantasy stories in order to camouflage emotional events because their emotions may be rooted in a reality too painful to express. If a child tells a story that you're not sure about, enjoy the tale for its own sake. Don't try to play amateur psychologist. Listen with a supporting manner and you will learn much.

The cultivation of imagination, story telling, and speech

is an important maturational step. How do we do it? The easiest and most direct method is to encourage children to make things up. This means going beyond these typical parental conversation stoppers:

"Where did you go?
"Out."
"What did you do?"
"Nothing."
"What happened in school today?"
"Not much."
"What did you learn?"
"Not much."
"Anything else you want to tell me?"
"No."

It should be noted that this kind of response is just as common among bright children as among dull children. The way around this is to sit with a child and begin by telling of interesting things that happened to you during the day. This encourages them to tell a story of their own. Then you can ask more directed questions:

- Did this ever happen to you?
- Why don't you like Joey?
- What would you do if you owned your own spaceship?
- If you had a fairy godmother, what would you ask her for? . . . Then what would you do?

Stay away from the inquisitorial style and let the spigot of words flow from the child. Remember that a large part of the child's reaction and response is based on the parent's reaction and response to the child. Be concrete. "How was your day?" is too abstract and won't work with children, and it carries a tone of artificiality as well. The dinner table is a particularly good time to attend to children's speech and to let them dominate the conversation with anything they want to talk about. Dinner is a leisurely meal and can become a regular forum for the child if parents can save their necessary conversation for later.

## READING

When a child tries to read what he has just written, he is using different cognitive skills than those used in the act of encoding the material in the first place. The presumption that a child learning to write can automatically read is a good and sound presumption, but it isn't a one-to-one match. As I listen to children decoding what they have written, it is clear to me that a different mental function is involved. It is apparently more difficult to extract sound from the visual representation of that sound. In addition, children are helped to learn to read by hearing their parents read and by being encouraged to "read along."

Initially, reading along is largely a memory task. The child follows the verbal words spoken by the parent and makes mental associations. Gradually, however, the child begins to look at the words in the book as well as the pictures and to recognize words. This normally happens when a favorite story has been selected and read and reread many times. This kind of recognition, the placing of the spoken word "bread" with the word symbol for *bread* on the page, represents the closing of the symbolic triangle.

# CHAPTER 11

# WRITING TO READ AT HOME: THE BASICS

WE HAVE COVERED the theory on which the Writing to Read System is based and the elements of the program as it works in the schools. The rest of this book will be devoted to specific suggestions on how parents can teach their children to write and read at home without all the accoutrements of the formal program and especially without the computer.

This portion of the book will be very prescriptive, almost like a cookbook, so that you, as parents, can teach your own child how to write before he or she can read. It isn't an easy task but it is a rewarding one, and both you and your child will benefit greatly from the effort.

In the first day of Writing to Read in the classroom the children are exposed to all the elements of the program, including the computer and the typewriter. People are always shocked when I tell them that in our classroom children even use the typewriter from the very first day. They can't believe that a child who scarcely knows the alphabet can spend any constructive time hunting for letters on the typewriter keyboard. The truth is, as we've said, that the typewriter is the perfect piece of equipment for early learning because it takes the work out of forming letters.

I'm highlighting the use of the typewriter on the first day of class as an example of the way our program integrates its elements and how, rather than trying to schedule learning in a linear progression, the activities take place concurrently. To expand on this point, because it is an important one, keep in mind that nothing in Writing to Read is in lieu of something else. There is always much more to do than can be done in one short learning session. Therefore, on any given day chalk and slate may be the only activity and on another it may be clay, or pencil and paper, or fingers in the sand. Because of the child's interest, however, fingers in the sand may go on for five straight days. You may suggest clay and have it rejected. You may select listening to the alphabet tape and have it rejected. In fact, the whole idea may be rejected for the day, and I wouldn't press the issue more than once before giving in to the child's wish to do nothing. As a parent, you know that it's probably not just a matter of whim or flightiness. The child may be coming down with a cold, and this rejection of the daily learning session is the first symptom that he is going to have a fever later in the day. On the other hand, if the rejection of the learning schedule goes on day after day without the sign of any illness, lay the entire program aside for a week or ten days and then come back to it with a fresh activity. The point is, there is no order of things that must be followed and equally as important, there is no hard and fast rule about progress.

There are some other basics to keep in mind, and we'll examine them now.


## PATIENCE

Children progress at different rates. This may sound simplistic, but few parents recognize the fact that their child is unique and should not be compared to any other child. There is an extraordinarily wide range of normalcy from the mentally adequate to the mentally superior, just as there is a wide range of normalcy in the physical development of children. It's perfectly within these ranges for one child to arrive at school able to read and write and for another to have little competency in either task. The same is true of size and weight. One child may be inches taller than another and weigh as much as forty pounds more, yet the range is normal. It is important to recognize and accept these variations.

All parents are rightfully concerned with the rapid educational advancement of their children, but our experience shows that some parents are impatient and too anxious to see progress. The demands of our society dictate that a child must get a good start in learning to write and read. This is the foundation for all academic learning. There are parents who, in their zeal to ensure a place for their children in the world of higher education and therefore in the world of work, file college applications at the time of birth. This strong parental desire for excellence in their children, regardless of its origins, can result in pressures on children to learn that are as damaging as they are unrealistic. Nowhere in my experience is patience more of a virtue than in teaching children.

## WORK SPACE

As an adult, you know that having your own work space at home is very important. It's a rare middle-class home that doesn't have some area designated as an office these days. It doesn't matter if it's the corner of the kitchen counter, a writing table in the living room, a desk in the bedroom, or a full-fledged office in the basement, as long as you can call it yours.

The same thing is true for your child. He or she needs to have a space—a table or a small desk—where working materials can be kept without fear that someone will come along and mess them up. The furniture in this work space should be child-sized—that is, the chair should be low enough for the child's feet to reach the floor and the desk height should be sized from twenty-two to twenty-four inches from the floor.

The space should also have good light and ventilation—in short, all those elements that make for a comfortable learning situation, the kind of space you would want for yourself. And it should be completely clear that this is the child's space.

## NECESSARY EQUIPMENT

You will need only two major pieces of equipment as you begin teaching your child to write and read at home, and both should be kept in the regular work space.

The first item is a tape recorder and a pair of earphones. You'll use the recorder at several points in the teaching process. It need not be an expensive model, and in fact, it's better if it isn't because it should be easy for a child to handle (less expensive recorders have fewer buttons) and you won't be worried about it being dropped or abused if it isn't costly to replace or repair. Inexpensive thirty-minute tape cassettes complete the package.

The most important piece of equipment you'll need is a typewriter, preferably one with a type-ball or a daisy-wheel printing element. If you don't have a good typewriter, then I suggest you buy one. There are many good models on the market for under $400. I realize that this represents a significant investment, but it is an investment in your child's learning future and it will be useful, not only for Writing to Read but for all members of the family. If the typewriter you select gives you the option, order a typing element with oversize letters, preferably fourteen-point type in Helvetica style. Children prefer the larger type size, and the Helvetica letters are clear and plain.

## ALPHABET BOOKS

There are many simple and inexpensive alphabet books available, and if you do not already have several, you should buy one. Historically, the most widely known of these was *The New England Primer,* but it is not very useful even for religious families. It begins with "A is for Adam, in whose fall we sinned all," good Puritan Calvinism. As a special project, you and your child can make this kind of book yourself if you remember two things that characterize the interests of little children:

- The world of fantasy is as real to a child, and maybe more appealing sometimes, than the real world. It's a place inhabited by ogres and giants and fairies and unicorns and elves and animated characters. So don't shy away from words that come from that wonderful world.
- Children are very comfortable on the edge of our developing culture. Television, the movies, real men on the moon, space satellites, and spacecraft are as normal to a child today as an airplane was fifty years ago. For today's child, spaceships, space travel, and the stars are close to their sense of reality.

Therefore, words and pictures drawn from the scientific side of our culture and the fantasy world will be very appealing to children as well as the everyday, real and familiar world of the kitchen. Magazines and newspapers provide all these kinds of words and pictures to illustrate and they are a fertile source for compiling your own alphabet books. Here is a sample of the words drawn from these two worlds that are appealing to children:

atom apple android arrow airplane
bazooka banana bat beanstalk blast
crater cavern chariot clock chimpanzee
dragon dream dwarf elephant eagle eye
egg fly fable frisbee gorilla ghost gift
horse hulk hang hotel ice cream iceberg
igloo input interstellar junk journey jump
jet king knight key karate laboratory
long legend lobster mother monster
mobile magic night noon nebula news
object octopus oil ocean panther planet
penny quiz quote question quarter rabbit
race red reveal run space star satellite
sea tape time tail ugly uncle uranium
victor voice vast world waste wicked
witch x ray yacht yoga yoke young zebra
zero zigzag zipper

## OTHER MATERIALS

The child's work area should also contain some or all of the following materials:

1.  An assortment of pencils, markers, pens, and paper. The pencils, as we've said, must be short, round, have soft lead, and have the erasers removed. If you can't find short pencils, buy those that are regular size and cut them in half. The markers should be darker colors (blue, black, green, red) that can easily be seen. The paper should be 8½-by-11-inch sheets, unlined and cut in half to form two sheets, 5½ by 8½ inches, because a full sheet is rarely filled. These writing implements will be used for a variety of writing and drawing tasks.

2.  A package of sticks of blue, gray, or red clay that will be rolled into thin strings and used to form letters and to match letters printed on paper. Light colors such as yellow will not give enough contrast. Hard clay is an irritant to children, so buy good-quality material and keep it in a plastic bag when not in use.

3.  A piece of slate and soft chalk. Oil base, or hard chalk, makes less dust, but it also makes a screech which bothers children. Like soft clay, soft chalk is a way of avoiding those minor irritations that can hinder learning. Most tile stores sell slate in pieces about twelve inches square. If you can't obtain it commercially, it is a simple matter to create your own slate. Use masking tape to block out a square space on the child's worktable or on a piece of plywood. Spray that area with flat black or green paint that is labeled for that purpose. Use two coats and allow overnight for drying. This dried-paint–slate surface will take chalk nicely and

erase just as easily as the real thing. A four-inch square of toweling is an excellent eraser.

4.  Two sets of the twenty-six letters of the alphabet, each letter on a piece of cardboard about two inches square. These letters can be purchased at many toy and bookstores. You can make your own set by drawing ¼-by-¾-inch black letters on cardboard with a felt pen. Then cut them to size. Make one set of capital letters and one set of lowercase letters. These will be used as guides for the shaping of letters out of clay rolled into strings. When your child uses them to line them up into words, you will need at least one extra set of the lowercase alphabet.

5.  A cassette tape of the alphabet song, which you make yourself. The song should be sung several times so that the tape does not have to be constantly rewound. It will be used with the alphabet letters or the alphabet book to solidify the idea that letters have names. Sing the song very slowly the first time and very gradually increase the speed as you repeat the song.

6.  File folders for the convenient collection of your child's work. Kept chronologically, a file will show you and your child how much progress is being made. This visible record of growth (you can put dates on each piece of paper) is a powerful stimulator for learning. Though they can't read your dating marks, they love to say, "When I was little, I couldn't do it. Now I can."

7.  Gather a variety of shoe-box-size containers for the pencils, markers, and the rest of the writing materials as well as for the cutout letters, the clay, and additional tapes that you may make. Everything should have its own place, so don't mix the chalk with the pencils, the letters with the clay, and so forth. Use open boxes or tin cans on which you may paste pictures of the contents when necessary.

## SOME OPTIONAL MATERIALS

There are two additional surfaces that are useful for teaching the letters of the alphabet. One of these consists of cutouts of the letters of the alphabet (both upper- and lowercase) made with fine-grained black emery cloth or sandpaper. These can be glued to a contrasting surface and make excellent tactile surfaces for the child's fingers to explore. Be warned. They are not easy to make.

The other tactile surface that is easier to create and serves a similar purpose is a shallow cooking tray about six by eight inches that has a sheet of the same fine-grained emery cloth glued to the bottom. Spread about one-quarter inch of sand, Jell-O powder, or farina on the bottom of the tray. Be sure not to put too much on the bottom because the sides of the letters will collapse. This surface is used to trace the letters of the alphabet and it's erasable by respreading the material with the hand or with a six-inch-long ruler. An interesting aside is that our work in the schools has shown that a significant number of teachers and children do not like this activity if sand is used. We don't know why this is, but we do know that sand makes more of a mess than rice or farina and this may be bothersome. So take the path of least resistance and use the material that is most acceptable to your child.

In our classrooms we have successfully used other sensory materials as well. The following items are available either in toy stores or discount stationery stores:

- Blocks with alphabet letters
- Individual rubber stamps (and stamp pads) with the letters of the alphabet
- Magnetic letters and magnetic boards
- Plastic letters
- Flannel boards with letters
- Anagram letters similar to those used in Scrabble.

All of these items are useful and they are relatively equal in manipulability, durability, and safety. A variety of formats and materials encourages children to continue to work with letters, and that is the important point. A choice also allows for the selection of activities that are particularly appealing at a given moment, but don't flood your child with a confusion of too many choices.

# CHAPTER 12

# WRITING TO READ AT HOME: HOW TO DO IT

### The Dinisor Book by Bill

Dinisaur are mēn. I don't like dinisaur. A dinisaur cum in all shaps and sises. Once in the lab all most evry bity ritid a dinisaur story. Dinisaur are very very mēn. Some dinisaurs are big sum are little. Dinasaur livd a long time. Dinisaur dont live nouw. Som dinisaur hāv horns some dont The bigist dinisaur is the one that livs in the seē. thiārs a reson no biy nos wȳ the dinisaur dīd.

### Story of goofy by Lamar

One day I went to goofy house and when I saw him he was biuding something. Then I said what are you biuding and he said games and stuff and I said what els. Then he said recker tapes and play money and books. And then I said lets play a game and he said okay and we did. Then a big storm came and bluew us rite out of goofy house and it did not stop until the end then it stoped and I said good. Then we was looking for a new house and we foud a golden house. It was good as new and we stade there. then goofy told me thank you and I said it was notthing and that was the end.

One day I found a kitn. The kitn was blak and yellow. I like the cat. But whin I gave the cat a pes ov thred the cat did not play with it. It was not so good. Then I gave it sum millk. But it still whud not drenk it. I did not now whut to do. Whut can I do. Then she startid to drenk the millk. I wos glad. Now I play with it a lot.

THESE ARE EXAMPLES of the type of work Writing to Read students produce in the classroom. Your child will be writing with the same facility as Bill and Lamar and the anonymous author of the story about the kitten. I can't tell you exactly how long it will take to reach this level, but I can tell you it will happen. Before we get into specific suggestions for working with your child and the types of exercises you will be doing, however, I think it's important that we review exactly what it is you will be teaching, how you will be teaching it, and what your child will be learning. It is not a good idea to explain this sequence of events to your child even in simple terms. Children will not comprehend these mechanics or even the words you use to describe the ideas to yourself, but they will be able to do these tasks before they can grasp and understand these essential elements.

## THE THINKING PROCESS

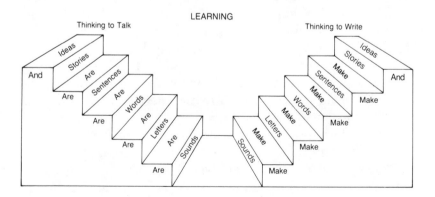

Study the illustration of these two "Thinking" staircases closely. When your child is "Thinking to Write," he or she will be moving up the stairs one at a time while working on the concepts involved. Having decided what is to be written and the words to express the thought, your child will "make" each word by learning these steps:

*Step 1:* The fact that letters make sounds

*Step 2:* Placed together in a line, those same letters make words

*Step 3:* Placed together in a line, those same words make sentences

*Step 4:* Placed together in logical sequence, those sentences make stories and those stories express ideas.

When "Thinking to Read," the sequence moves in the opposite direction and follows these steps:

*Step 1:* Stories and ideas are made of sentences placed together in a logical sequence

*Step 2:* Sentences are made of words placed in a row

*Step 3:* Words are made up of letters placed in a row

*Step 4:* Letters are made of sounds.

We usually think that learning must progress from step to step—that is, step A leads to step B, step B leads to step C, and so on. In the Writing to Read System progress is not made in a straight line. In fact, though most of us were brought up on the idea that it is necessary to pile up learning like a series of building blocks until the structure is completed, linear progressions are not necessary in most of learning because the brain does not have to move in a sequence. Therefore, keep in mind that you need not move rigidly through these stair steps, up one staircase and down the other. The movement will be necessarily erratic because children, like adults, don't learn skills in a linear manner. The learning of one element will take place simultaneously and in parallel with the learning of other elements. There-

fore, your child will be doing all of the following, but these
activities will overlap:

- Learning sounds
- Labeling things with words
- Telling stories verbally
- Listening to stories
- Writing the letters of the alphabet
- Arranging letter cards to form words
- Making letter sounds
- Writing words
- Writing sentences
- Writing stories
- Typing words and sentences
- Working with sensory materials.

Now review the principles of Writing to Read for yourself.

## THE ALPHABETIC PRINCIPLE

You may want to review what we said about the alphabetic principle in chapter 1, but it will be enough to
remember that the alphabetic principle is the practice of
combining the twenty-six letters of the alphabet in various
ways to form words. Help your child understand the advanced intellectual skill and insight that is represented by
the formulation of the alphabet itself. Point out that before
we developed our twenty-six letters, the only way people
communicated by writing was with picture representations
of everything they wanted to write. That meant that writing
took thousands of pictures and was slow. Only a few people,
called scribes, were able to do it with skill. As the centuries
passed, people's drawings became less and less representational and more like the abstract form of art characterized
by the Chinese ideogram. Finally our current alphabet
evolved, using only twenty-six letters to write all the words,

thousands of them, and the entire process of human communication was changed.

## PHONEMIC SPELLING

The English spelling system has evolved during the past 1,500 years using the twenty-six letters in various combinations, but the way in which words are spelled today has become inconsistent with the alphabetic principle about half of the time, so that most of the rules about how to spell work only part of the time, and in many cases there are no rules at all for certain irregular situations. This is very confusing to adults and children learning to write and read English; therefore, for Writing to Read we've developed a phonemic system, a simplified alphabet, a way of spelling that consists of forty-two letter-sounds, which we call phonemes. All spoken words can be put on paper using these phonemes. Though they may not be spelled absolutely correctly, they can be easily read and understood. For this reason, it is not important if a word is spelled correctly at this early stage of learning. What is important is that children understand that they can put a word together by putting symbols on paper, letters that represent the sounds they make when they speak that word—any word.

In Writing to Read we begin the lessons in Cycle 1 with the words *cat*, *dog*, and *fish*. The second cycle has the words *pig*, *sun*, and *bed*. In these six words there are fifteen different phonemes (single letters and combinations, such as "sh" in *fish*) out of the total of forty-two such sounds we use. The letters representing these sounds are the building blocks of words. These letter-for-sound symbols help children realize that the sounds of speech can be written and that if they can say a word they can write it. This is a delightful revelation for children. When they are able to understand that to write is to represent the sounds that come out of their mouths as they speak, an important step has been taken on the road to writing. We call this "talking with your fingers on paper."

## WRITING LEADS TO READING

To begin to combine letter-sounds to form words, children need to realize that letters stand for sounds and that words are composed of those letter-sounds. Your child will first encounter reading when he reads back the words that have been "talked" onto the paper. This leads directly to the idea that words on paper are no more than thoughts written down, spoken words that can be seen. Thus, as children learn how to write what they can say, they also learn how to read what they have written, and they understand that these two processes are interrelated.

## MULTI-SENSORY LEARNING

Writing to Read uses all the senses to stimulate the learning process. Don't neglect these aspects of the program. It is just as important to make letters out of clay strings as it is to sit at the typewriter and hunt and peck letters and words. It is as important to say the letters of the alphabet out loud as it is to write them. It is as important to talk as it is to listen, and it is important to hear stories either read by a parent or on tape. All the senses bring information to the brain. To touch, to feel, to shape, to hear, and to see are all preludes to thinking, talking, and writing.

## THE TIME FACTOR

There are three questions of time involved in learning by the Writing to Read System:

1. How long does the program take?
2. How long should you work with your child at one sitting?
3. How often and when during the day should you work with your child?

There is no definitive answer to any of these questions that will be right for every child, but there are some guidelines that hold true for many children most of the time. Unfortunately, there are no guidelines that are true for all children all the time.

Your child may be a very mature four-year-old or a slowly developing five-year-old. To talk, as many books do, about four-year-olds and five-year-olds as though there are unique and distinctive things that are true for all fours and all fives is to imply what may be false in terms of any one child. Four-year-olds differ from each other and from five-year-olds in height, weight, speech development, and every other aspect of their maturation. Girls, as early as age five, are a year ahead of boys physiologically; they have larger vocabularies and respond to the process of learning to write and to read more readily and with higher aptitude than boys the same age. If you have a girl, you can anticipate easier and faster learning. If you have a boy, things could take a little longer. Given these facts and the fact that learning aptitudes vary greatly themselves, we will describe central tendencies. Remember that the largest four-year-old will be taller than the average five-year-old, and the smallest normal five-year-old will be shorter than the average four-year-old. The range of "normal" is very large.

Therefore, from day one to the ability to write very simple sentences, and to the first flashes of understanding that by stringing those sentences together a story can be told, this whole process of learning writing and reading will vary from child to child. It may take less than three months for some acute five-year-old children. There will be some children who will make very little progress even after fifteen or eighteen months. We know this is true from our observations of thousands of children. The advantage of a parent, working one-on-one with their own child, may produce results equal to, or better than, that gained in the school. But the range of three months to eighteen months is still probably the time span needed to include more than 90 percent of children.

It's sometimes hard for parents to understand this broad range of progress, but you need only recall that the onset of puberty is normal between the ages of ten and twenty-one. We like to think it's normal if it occurs at twelve years plus or minus a little, but the truth is that the range is extremely broad and many youngsters don't reach puberty until their late teens.

The second part of the time question, how long to work each day, is more definable. The answer is, as long as it stays pleasant and fun. But if you work to the point where it's no longer pleasant and fun for either child or parent, you've already worked too long.

There are several ways to keep a session from running too long:

- Recognize that fifteen to twenty minutes is enough and that thirty minutes borders on excess.
- Begin with the idea of only one activity each day but don't hesitate to change if joyful enthusiasm starts to drop.
- Stop an activity arbitrarily when you can sense that a peak has been reached and is starting to fall. Don't allow it to drag on and drain the child of energy and drain you of your patience, to the point where an edge creeps into your voice at the same time your child is getting edgy, fretsome, and fatigued.
- Listen and watch for signals from your child; eye rubbing, messiness, a snappy response all indicate tiring.
- In general young children exhibit energy in proportion to their interest.
- Simply say, "That's enough for today," when you realize it is time to quit.

Causing a child to stop when he wants to go on leaves him and you with a desire to return the next day. It is infinitely better than allowing him to continue to the point where things get pushed aside or spilled because of fatigue. Interestingly, fatigue may occur for four-year-olds after ten minutes, for fives after fifteen minutes. One second the child

is alert, alive, and receptive, and the next he or she is tired
and recalcitrant. Above all, you want their last memory of
the activity to be one of happy anticipation, not one of dis-
gruntlement because things have been allowed to go on
beyond the limit of the child's interest and energy level. I
have found that adults tend not to recognize the fact that
children expend an enormous amount of energy when they
are focused and involved. They are capable of a tremendous
amount of energy, but it is not unlimited.

Also be aware of the fact that a child who is about to
come down with a cold, or one who is just recovering from
one, will not have his usual concentration and intensity.
One of the signs of a coming illness is a fretsome child, the
glazed eye, the pale coloring. Concentration and the ability
to absorb is greatly diminished at these times. All parents
learn this, but it is necessary to remember that a coming
cold can interfere with learning.

The third time element involved is when and how often
to work with your child. The answer is every day at the
same time, whenever that may be.

Keep in mind that children like to be organized. They
like to know when and where something is supposed to
happen. They may not be able to tell time by the clock but
they have a sense of time. It is important, therefore, to
maintain a daily schedule of learning activities. This means
seven days a week and a definite effort to work at the same
time every day. On the weekends you may need to make
adjustments or drop sessions in order to fulfill other obli-
gations. In two-parent households, however, the second parent may take responsibility on weekends. By all means try
not to postpone the weekday sessions. Your preschool child
is not particularly aware that weekends are different from
other days, and continuity is a prime element in learning.

Set a regular time for your meeting and make it a routine. If this is an after-breakfast activity it should be an
after-breakfast activity every day; if it's scheduled for af-
ternoon or after dinner it should be done at the same time
every day. You know your young child best, and you know
the times when he or she is particularly alert and active.
Those are the times to choose for your sessions. A tired or

cranky child will not learn well when he or she needs a nap, and may develop an aversion to working with you on these activities if you decide to try to work at those times.

If a child, of his or her own volition, wants to go into the work space and work with some of the materials or play the alphabet song at a different time in addition to your regular session, you certainly should not forbid it, but maintain your scheduled routine as well.

The child's frame of mind is important here, but of course, a good deal depends on the frame of mind of the parent as well. You are going to become fatigued too. There will be days when you don't feel like working, and on those days it's best to cut your time short or postpone your work schedule altogether. When the child knocks the tray of sand onto the floor, you will have to control your desire to say something negative and keep things from becoming unpleasant. This should be easier for you to do than for the child, but if you have never taught, it will take some practice and self-control. Don't be timid in setting standards. Use the sudden decision to stop the session as a disciplinary device. The tray of sand on the floor is such an occasion. And finish each day with the strict requirement to put everything back in order.

## SOME OTHER GUIDELINES ON WORKING WITH YOUR CHILD

We have spoken of cultivating patience with your child's pace of learning and accepting the fact that not all children learn at the same rate. Well, patience is also required on a day-to-day basis in the learning sessions themselves. The extraordinarily wide range of normal response makes it impossible to speak of single ways to respond to your children's successes and errors. Besides, it would be a mechanical way to work with children and that's not our method. But within that wide range, here are some suggestions:

- It's almost always true that if the activity isn't fun or interesting for you, it isn't likely to be fun or interesting for your child. If it is a chore and a duty for you, then the child is going to react by saying to himself, "The only reason I'm doing this is because my mother wants me to." That is a reason, but if it is the only reason, it isn't a good one.

- The best measure of the rightness of what's happening is the child's sense of satisfaction about doing it. So if a child is focused on a task, that satisfaction is due to the appropriateness of that activity.

- A thing learned today may well be forgotten tomorrow or the next day and will have to be relearned. This is perfectly normal and it is true of adults as well as children, but it is something that you will have to understand and get used to. Your child will repeat the same thing many times before it is finally learned.

- A four-year-old will generally not make aesthetically pleasing letters or even marks that are close to your idea of the letter intended. What the child calls the letter $a$ may be indistinguishable to you from a scribble. But if the child thinks it is an $a$, then you accept it. Similar scribbles will occur whether the work is done on paper, in sand, or with clay. You may want to make your version of an $a$ next to the child's for a model, but that is all that need be done.

- The above continues to be true as your child becomes older and it may still be true at age five and even beyond. What the child perceives in these scribbles we don't know. It may well be that between the perception of the letter and the dexterity to make that letter there is a gap that only maturity can close.

- The recognition of the real shape of letters is gradual and it takes place naturally over a period of weeks or even months.

- Don't be impatient for learning to take place. We can't see learning happen in the brain, but we do know that it takes time for the brain to connect all the pieces of learning into a new understanding.

## HOW TO CORRECT YOUR CHILD'S ERRORS

We have spoken of the delicacy of the child's psyche and we have mentioned that correcting children can be a subtle form of abuse. We know that it isn't intended as such, but it can have that effect. Correcting can also be the manifestation of the adult's need to maintain control over the child and the learning process.

In our experience in the classroom we have discovered methods of correcting children's mistakes that accomplish the job with a minimum of immediate trauma. Here are some things to keep in mind:

- The way to understand a child's reaction to correction is to look into yourself and ask yourself how well you take correction. The answer is probably that you don't take it very well, because not many of us do. If you realize that being corrected hurts your feelings and sensitivities, you will realize that it hurts the feelings and sensitivities of little children.
- In the formative stages, when the child quite seriously makes an *a* and it looks like tangled spaghetti on the page, there is no good way to correct it without being critical and producing a negative reaction. Don't change the child's effort at making the letter, regardless of how it appears; continually write the letter correctly to show him or her a model of what is correct.
- When working with your child, use phrases similar to these: "I can't read that letter. Tell me what it is." "Try writing it again. Maybe I'll be able to read it."
- It doesn't produce any immediate results to say, "Do it this way." Instead, say, "This is how I do

it." The child may be ready to recognize the difference, and his or her ability to make the letter correctly will begin to develop.

- Don't indicate to your child that you are discouraged with the way things are going. Comments like "We just went over that" are just as abrasive as saying, "That's not the way to do it."

- The period of time required for the development of these skills, which demand both mental and manual dexterity, is usually only a matter of weeks. If it takes longer than this and there is no joy in the lessons, then perhaps the whole program is premature. If you judge that this is the case, then put it aside for several months.

- Any task that is beyond the immediate skill level should be postponed because it will result in errors and more frustration.

- Remember that learning varies from child to child and for each child from day to day.

## FOUR ADDITIONAL POINTS TO KEEP IN MIND

**Point One:** We are so used to hearing, understanding, and learning in what we consider a linear fashion—that is, this leads to the next thing, and the next thing leads to the next—that we find it hard to change and accept another way of looking at things. Linearity is a valid concept, of course, but in learning complex skills like writing and reading, children learn as we described in our staircase illustration on p. 129. They learn the risers and treads on this staircase irregularly and concurrently. Learning takes place in a series of parallel activities. A child can learn the symbols for sounds while listening to and understanding stories. Making closure in that sequence of understanding comes later, because the child is walking mentally on several pathways at once. Therefore, you can be illogical in your approach to a logical progression. You may decide to use one thing ahead of another, this today and something else tomorrow, in any random order that makes sense to you as you and your child work together.

**Point Two:** Children like to draw pictures. This begins early in their development and goes on continuously for a long time. These drawings, which often appear to be only a mass of spaghetti lines, a bunch of swirls and circles and some ups and downs, mean something specific to the child. With a straight face you can ask what it is and the answer will be something like "That's Grandma," or "That's me," "That's a dog," "That's an airplane," "That's a circus," "That's the earth," "Those are stars," or whatever the child's imagination calls for. This answer may actually be what the child intended to draw or merely an invention in response to your question. But truth or fantasy, all children do this kind of preliminary writing, and it may continue until age five and after. Encourage this sort of self-expression.

**Point Three:** When you begin the vocabulary building activities described below, you will be labeling cards with letters and words. Don't worry about having more than one syllable in a word. Your child won't be reading syllables or letters. He will be seeing the word and will recognize it by length or profile, something like one would recognize a hieroglyph. For example, the word *dog* has a different profile than the word *book*. *Refrigerator* and *television* are recognizable by their length. The length of a word is not as important as its familiarity.

**Point Four:** As we said, it's perfectly normal for both children and adults seemingly to master something today and forget it tomorrow. Some things must be relearned and relearned and relearned. In the case of learning to write and read, it isn't a question of your impatience or a child being obstinate, it is that children's minds work like pendulums. They swing toward accomplishment and then retreat. They swing forward (sometimes not as far as before) and then retreat again; then forward and back a little, then forward, and then forward again. When real mastery takes place, a child reaches a level of almost autonomic learning, a point where the child no longer has to think to write an old word that has been learned many times. At this level the word *sink* or *cat* or *house* is written without the need for the child to say to himself that this is the alphabetic representation of the sounds I make when I speak that word.

Once more, the child-parent activities we are going to describe do have an order, but as a parent you must be free to help the child work with these activities as you both feel appropriate. The absorption by the child of the whole logical process is best accomplished by a seemingly random combination of activities over a period of months in which the letters of the alphabet are handled at times as if they only had names and at others as if they had sounds and at other times as whole words.

## TEACHING PHONEMES

Since learning the forty-two phonemes is basic to our program, you have to begin here. The easiest way to present these sounds is through pictures of common objects that are already known to your child. You can get all the illustrations you need by cutting pictures from magazines and newspapers that illustrate the phonemes. Paste the pictures on slightly larger sheets of cardboard. Use the phoneme chart on the opposite page to make sure that you have illustrations to cover all the sounds.

Use a felt-tip pen and write the name of the object on the cardboard border or on a piece of paper in lowercase letters and glue the name to the picture. Then follow the manner of presentation of the material that we discussed in detail in chapter 2. It is a good idea to refer back to that section for a review. Obviously, you will now have to serve the function of the computer and the tape recorder. That is: You will say the phoneme, then say the word, then say the phoneme, and then the word, and so on. As you say the

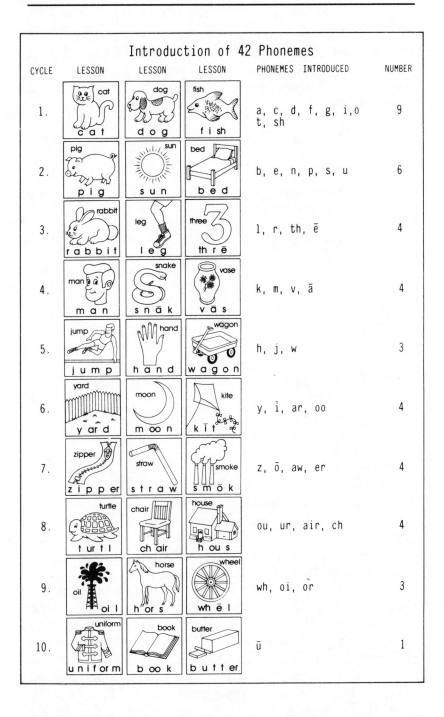

## Introduction of 42 Phonemes

| CYCLE | LESSON | LESSON | LESSON | PHONEMES INTRODUCED | NUMBER |
|-------|--------|--------|--------|---------------------|--------|
| 1. | cat — c a t | dog — d o g | fish — f i sh | a, c, d, f, g, i, o t, sh | 9 |
| 2. | pig — p i g | sun — s u n | bed — b e d | b, e, n, p, s, u | 6 |
| 3. | rabbit — r a b b i t | leg — l e g | three — th r ē | l, r, th, ē | 4 |
| 4. | man — m a n | snake — s n ā k | vase — v ā s | k, m, v, ā | 4 |
| 5. | jump — j u m p | hand — h a n d | wagon — w a g o n | h, j, w | 3 |
| 6. | yard — y ar d | moon — m oo n | kite — k ī t | y, ī, ar, oo | 4 |
| 7. | zipper — z i p er | straw — s t r aw | smoke — s m ō k | z, ō, aw, er | 4 |
| 8. | turtle — t ur t l | chair — ch air | house — h ou s | ou, ur, air, ch | 4 |
| 9. | oil — oi l | horse — h or s | wheel — wh ē l | wh, oi, or | 3 |
| 10. | uniform — u n i f or m | book — b oo k | butter — b u t t er | ū | 1 |

phoneme, have your child repeat what you say. We'll use
the word *cat* as an example. You should write the word *cat*
on the top and bottom borders of a picture of a cat. Remember, you will be saying the sounds of the letters, not the
names of the letters in this exercise. Here is how it goes:

| PARENT | CHILD |
|---|---|
| Say cat | cat |
| Say c (say the sound of c, not its name) | c |
| Say a (as it is in *cat*) | a |
| Say t (as it is in *cat*) | t |
| Say cat | cat |
| Say cat | cat |
| Say c | c |
| Type (or write) c | c |
| Say cat | cat |
| Say a | a |
| Type (or write) a | a |
| Say cat | cat |
| Say t | t |
| Say cat | cat |
| Type (or write) cat | cat |

The number of repetitions of the word and the phonemes given above should only be used as a guide, but you
should present the material in this order. You may want to
repeat each of them several more times. It won't hurt to
repeat, but the first time you say a letter you should point
at the letter, and each time you say the word *cat* you should
point at the picture of the cat. The next time ask your child
to point with you. Remember to go slowly, to pronounce the
sounds carefully, and to repeat as many times as you think
necessary. At this stage it is unimportant for your child to
be able to write the letters of *cat* individually or to write
the word *cat* correctly. The beginning recognition of the
sounds of the phonemes is the critical skill to be learned
here, but begin to use the typewriter the very first day. Let
your child look for and type the letters as you and he or she

say their sounds. This is a learning experience for the child, so don't point to the letters immediately. Wait and wait some more before you point to the correct key. We realize that you will not be able to respond the same way the computer does—with no response at all—because this will not indicate to the child that an incorrect letter has been struck. It is only necessary that you say "Try again" in an even tone. Be prepared to repeat and repeat "Try again" without changing your tone.

As you can see, *cat* has three of the forty-two phonemes. You will have to repeat this process until each of the phonemes has been verbalized and written. As you continue with new words, you will find that some of the phonemes you have covered will show up again. When that is the case, they should be repeated as if they were new. Let's take another example that already includes the phoneme *c* as in *cat*.

| PARENT | CHILD |
|---|---|
| Say cup | cup |
| Say c | c |
| Say u | u |
| Say p | p |
| Say cup | cup |
| Say cup | cup |
| Say c | c |
| Type c | c |
| Say cup | cup |
| Say u | u |
| Type u | u |
| Say cup | cup |
| Say p | p |
| Type p | p |
| Say cup | cup |
| Type cup | cup |

Note that the phoneme *c* is treated as if it were being seen for the first time. Maintain this pattern throughout because it serves two functions: It maintains consistency and it reinforces the recognition of the phoneme when it reoccurs.

It is best to work on only one word each day, and you may find that it takes more than one day to finish a word. As soon as you feel that the phonemes are being seen as letters, move on to the next word and then the next. After you have completed three words, go back and conduct your own Mastery Test (see chapter 3) to see if your child has picked up the sounds and if some skill is developing in typing or writing those sounds.

Your job is to keep each lesson on the right track, to help your child focus attention on the task at hand, to be encouraging but not sugary, and to see that progress is being made.

## CONCURRENT ACTIVITIES

Try to imagine the Writing to Read classroom we explained earlier. Remember that it had places for the computers, the typewriters, the sensory materials, and a reading-listening center. Remember, too, that all those things were there to be used at the same time the computer was doing the teaching of the phonemes. Your home learning center, while not as complete, should be used in the same way.

So at the same time you are working on these initial words, your child should be using the typewriter, the sand tray, the clay, the markers, crayons, slate and chalk, tape recorder, and all the other materials you have gathered. This doesn't mean that he or she should work at every activity every day but that these things be available and that attention be switched from activity to activity.

Once you've explained the purpose and use of this cafeteria of fun activities, you do not have to supervise every move. What you must do, however, is make certain that the child is using them to reach the goal of learning how to write.

All of these activities are designed to teach the alphabet and expand on the idea of using phonemes to write the sounds that the child is able to say.

Keep in mind that the most attractive letters of all are those in your child's name, so you may want to begin each activity by using those letters. Here are some ways to use the materials we've been talking about.

## THE ALPHABET SONG

| | a | b | c | d | e | f | g | |
|---|---|---|---|---|---|---|---|---|
| h | i | j | k | l | m | n | o | p |
| | q | r | s | t | u | v | | |
| | w | x | y | and | z | | | |
| now | | I | know | my | a | b | | c's |
| tell | me | | what | you | think | | of | me |

Learning the names of the twenty-six letters of the alphabet will come easily if a child is presented with enough opportunities to identify and manipulate those letters. One ancient and effective method of teaching these letter names is the "Alphabet Song." Pointing to the letters as they are sung further develops the connection between the symbol and its name.

You can record this familiar song on tape so your child can listen to it and sing along. (Be sure to record it several times so that the tape will not have to be continuously rewound.) This is a pleasant and simple way for a child to experience the letters and of establishing the sequenced order of the letters in the child's mind.

## OTHER SONGS

Reading and singing nursery rhymes and children's songs has universal appeal. Children up to five years old and beyond like the sound and the cadence of such favorites as

"Baa Baa Black Sheep," "Three Blind Mice," "Old Mac-
Donald," and many others. These have been sung for hundreds
of years, and they have validity for learning because they
add to a child's sense of language. They shouldn't be neglected. You can buy tape-recorded versions of these classics, but you can also use the tape recorder to make your
own version. You may even want to sing and record them
with your child.

## READING

These same songs can be read as well as sung, and
there are hundreds of nursery rhymes and children's stories
that are not only enjoyable but also useful for learning the
alphabet and other reading and writing skills. Many of these
are also available on audio cassettes and they can provide
hours of pleasure for any child. You'll find that after listening to a tape several times, the child will soon begin mouth-
ing the words to the rhyme or story and eventually will say
and sing those words out loud with the tape. Encourage
your child to do so.

Here is an abbreviated list of some children's classics:

| TITLE | AUTHOR | PUBLISHER |
| --- | --- | --- |
| A Tree Is Nice | Janice May Udry | Harper & Row |
| Blueberries for Sal | Robert McCloskey | Viking-Penguin |
| The Emperor's Clothes | Hans C. Andersen | Houghton Mifflin |
| Little Bear's Visit | Else H. Minarik | Harper & Row |
| The Little House | Virginia L. Burton | Houghton Mifflin |
| The Little Red Hen | Paul Galdone | Houghton Mifflin |
| Make Way for Ducklings | Robert McCloskey | Viking-Penguin |
| Mike Mulligan | Virginia L. Burton | Houghton Mifflin |
| Mine's the Best | Crosby Bonsail | Harper & Row |
| Puddle to the Sea | Holling C. Holling | Houghton Mifflin |

| Peter's Chair | Ezra Jack Keats | Harper & Row |
| The Snowy Day | Ezra Jack Keats | Viking-Penguin |
| Socks for Supper | Jack Kent | Parents Magazine |
| The Three Bears | Paul Galdone | Houghton Mifflin |
| Thump and Plunk | Janice May Udry | Harper & Row |

You can add virtually all of the Dr. Seuss books to this list as well as those of Maurice Sendak, particularly *Where the Wild Things Are.* Though some adults think Sendak is too frightening for children, children themselves love his books and drawings. This is also a good chance to make use of your local library. They not only have the books, and sometimes the tapes, that you will want, but they have staff people who are well versed in children's literature of all kinds and who will go out of their way to help you.

## ALPHABET CARDS AND CLAY

To prepare for this activity use a dark, quarter-inch-wide felt-tip pen to trace lowercase outlines of the letters of the alphabet on unlined, white, three-by-five-inch index cards. Have several bars of dark-colored, very malleable clay on hand.

Show your child how to break off a small piece of clay, roll it into a ball, and then roll it out like a snake until it forms a long string. Take a card, perhaps the first letter of the child's name, and show your child how to place these clay strings over the letter on the card and point out how the clay actually forms that letter. The finished clay letter can be slipped off the card and set aside while the next letter in the child's name is formed in the same way. It will take a while to complete a child's name; Joe and Elizabeth have different tasks. But eventually the whole alphabet should be completed with the clay in this manner. Remember, your child's dexterity is not as good as yours, so to help, work along with your child making the strings. If no help is asked for, let the child make his own.

At the end of each session with the clay, make sure it is rolled into a ball and stored in a plastic bag or small container with a snap-on top.

## SANDPAPER LETTERS

This is an activity that gives the child another opportunity to experience the letters of the alphabet through the sense of touch, and the chance to write the letters at the same time. Cut two-inch-high lowercase letters of the alphabet out of fine sandpaper and glue them on slightly larger cards cut from three-by-five-inch index cards. Have either chalk and slate or pencil and paper available as well, whichever your child prefers.

Begin with the letters of his name. Have your child trace the letter with a forefinger several times. While he is tracing it, have him say the name of the letter out loud. You may have to say it first and then ask your child to repeat it.

Then attempt to transfer the pattern made with the finger (that neurological imprint) to the slate with chalk or to the paper using a pencil. Each time the letter is written it should be named: *a*, *b*, *c*, and so on. Each letter can be practiced over and over as long as it remains interesting for you and for your child. Move through the entire alphabet using only lowercase letters and then repeat the process using only the capital letters. Then do them side by side.

## SAND TRAY

The sand tray (you can use rice, farina, or even gelatin rather than sand if you wish) is another tactile exercise that deepens the imprint of letters and their sounds in a child's mind. This tray (constructed as described on p. 126) is used in much the same way as the sandpaper letters, but it erases easily and allows for quick changes from one letter to another.

As the child says the letter, he or she traces the shape of that letter in the sand. Again, each letter can be repeated as many times as the child wants or until interest lags.

## VOCABULARY BUILDING—MAKING WORDS

In our program the primary purpose of vocabulary building is to help the child learn the alphabetic principle that letters stand for the sounds they make when speaking. The activities we are suggesting here help a child discover that the letters they are learning in the phoneme sessions can be recombined to form completely new words.

Common household words offer a wonderful opportunity for doing this. Cut strips of oaktag (the kind of paper used for file folders) into three-by-six-inch pieces. Use a magic marker type of felt-tip pen for labeling. A pencil or fine-point pen isn't as readable. Use only lowercase letters and make them at least one inch high.

Now prepare labels with words like *table, chair, glass, refrigerator, oven, stove, spoon, knife, fork*, or any other common household item you choose. Six words will be enough initially. Spell them correctly. The game—and it's important to keep it as much of a game as possible—is to gather up the labels like a deck of cards and then have the child place the words (with your help) on or next to the item they name. As the groups of words are learned, you merely add new ones. This exercise shows a child that a thing can have a name and the name can be visible, which is a kind of "whole word" reading. When a few sets of words are mastered (two days of use without any major errors will indicate mastery), the idea may become tiresome for the child, and if this seems to be the case, just put it away for use at another time. If the child is still interested, by all means continue.

A variation on this game is to focus attention on one room, the child's bedroom for example. Here the choice of words includes *bed, dresser, closet, mirror, light, window, sheets*, and whatever else you want to add. Then, again with your help, ask your child to put the words together to make up, in this case, a bedroom story. The same can be done in the kitchen, bathroom, or living room. The story might come out something like this:

> I went into my room and turned on the *light*. Then I opened the *closet door*. I took a *shirt* out of the *dresser*. And I took a pair of *pants* [or a *dress*] out of the *closet*. And I took out my *shoes* too. I put them all on. I looked at myself in the *mirror*. Then I looked out the *window*.

## SCRAMBLED LETTERS

In this game, children form words using cards that have the letters of the alphabet written on them. You will need to make a complete set of alphabet letters and devise a convenient method of storing them so that your child has easy access to the letter he needs. Since several words will be made at a time, you will need about six of each of the vowels and at least two of each of the consonants.

You can make your own letters using pieces of cardboard or oaktag about one and a half inches square with one-inch letters written broadly in lowercase with a dark magic marker. The important thing is that they should be easy to find and to manipulate. Don't just dump them into a box where the task of finding the right letter, faceup or facedown, is a difficult job in itself. We've found that a plastic holder used for 35-mm photographic slides (available at any photo store) is good for the storage of these letters. It has slots that are big enough to hold several letters and it keeps them neat and ready. The storage system is vital because the job of visually matching is hard for the child and uses large quantities of mental energy. If you have an adult word game like Scrabble, the pieces from that game, though a little small, will work well in this exercise.

Here's how this game works. Begin with a picture of a common object like a hat. Use magazines and newspapers for your illustrations, and if you think it will make things clearer, you can mount the pictures on plain white sheets of paper. Then write on a piece of paper the letters *h*, *a*, and *t* with space between the letters, and glue this piece of paper onto the front of the picture.

As the guide, you have to be the articulator of the correct letter-sounds that match the letters in *hat*. You say the sound of the first letter, *h* in this case, and then have your child say it. Then the child has to find the letter that matches that sound. If the child has difficulty, continue to repeat the letter and if necessary point to the correct alphabet letter in the holder. Repeat the letter as many times as necessary. Continue this process with each letter of the word until the entire word *hat* is assembled either on the table under the picture or on the picture itself. Say the word *hat* at every opportunity.

This is the way we use the computer in teaching Writing to Read in the classroom. Refer back to the pattern suggested above. You, acting as computer, say the word, the letter sounds, the word, the sounds, and so forth.

It's important that you always begin with the concept —the hat or the dog or the tree or whatever. In the beginning it isn't the distinct letters *h*, *a*, *t*, but the concept "hat" that is important. It's the picture of the hat, the word *hat*, and then disassembling and reassembling the word which show the child the alphabetic principle that the word *hat* is made up of pictures of the same symbols of the same sounds you say when you say the word *hat*. When a person says "hat," it actually goes like this: You say "h," you say "a," you say "t." They are three separate sounds spoken as one flow of sound melded together. To disassemble the word and its sounds and to put them on paper is to use the symbols for those sounds. Because of this progression you should be sure to include the phonemes that combine two letters such as *sh*, *ar*, *wh*, and the others.

Children can learn this rather quickly. One day as I watched, a kindergarten child finished writing the word *fish* on the computer, and I followed him to his Work Journal, where he wrote *f*, *i*, *s*, *h*. I put my finger under the word and asked what he'd written. He said proudly that he had written *fish*. I put my finger under the *f* and asked what sound it was. He said the letter name, *f*. I said, "That's its name. That's right. But what sound does it make?" He thought for a moment and finally said with a spray, "ffff." I skipped over the *i* because vowel sounds are difficult for children to learn in these early stages, and I put my finger under the *sh*. I said, "What are those?" You could "see" him thinking. He was rejecting the impulse to name them. He thought again and said, "That one says 's-s-s' and that one says 'huh.'" I said, "That's great, but what happens when you say them together?" He thought and thought again and then he said triumphantly, "That says 'be quiet.'" This is an extraordinary intellectual feat children can accomplish. Not only did the *sh* make sounds, but the sounds themselves have a meaning. This child went to a fourth layer of understanding: from the name of the letters, to the sounds of the letters separately, to the sounds of the letters in combination, to the lovely accident that those particular sounds have the meaning of "be quiet."

## SCRAMBLED LETTERS—A VARIATION

This is a take-turns form of the scrambled letters game. Select a letter from the container that holds the alphabet letters used in the previous exercise and say to your child, "I'm going to make an *a*. You then write the letter *a* in lowercase on a sheet of white, unlined paper. Next suggest that your child make the same letter by saying, "Now you make an *a*." Try not to be any more directive than is necessary.

Now it is the child's turn. The dialogue should go something like this:

PARENT:   Which letter do you want to make?
CHILD:    I want to make a *d*.
PARENT:   Good. When you finish, I'll make a *d* also.
CHILD:    I made a *d*.
PARENT:   Now I'm going to make a *d*. . . . I made a *d* and now I'm going to make an *m*.

The first player names the letter and then makes the letter. Then the other person does the same. This is a co-operative effort. And by the way, it's important to remember that all of these lessons are done by you with your child. Depending on your child's maturing ability, go on with the game by including the letters in words used before so that *h* appears in *hat* and *d* in *dog* and so on.

## THE TYPEWRITER

The typewriter is such a valuable learning device that we suggest bringing it into your routine from the very first word, in fact, before the first word. At the same time you're playing alphabet games and singing alphabet songs, you can ask your child to find *a*, *b*, *c* on the typewriter. This is an important reinforcer of the sound-symbol idea. Letters can be typed perfectly in alphabetical order or at random, and they should be named while they are being typed. All of this fits into the same progression we're trying to develop with the use of clay, sand, chalk, and the rest of the materials.

To prepare paper for the typewriter, fold plain, white 8½-by-11-inch sheets twice to produce quarter sheets. Cut them and make a pile of paper next to the machine. This size sheet is easy for a child to handle and it makes your paper go further.

You demonstrate, and then ask your child to practice putting the paper in the typewriter vertically. Since all early typing is done in columns, it makes sense to offer a long, narrow sheet rather than a short, broad one. Use double spacing because it's easier for children to read. Set the margin to fit the sheet—about one half inch left and right. It's perfectly all right if your child types more than one word on a line or the same word repetitiously without spaces between the words. If several words do appear on the same line, there may not be any space between words (*catdogfish*, for example), but don't worry—that is also the way children talk. After the child has learned to hunt and peck his name, you can suggest that he type it on a line by itself at the top of each sheet of paper. This lends a special note of pride to the work. To keep a record, type or write the date. Later your child will learn to type his name and date as the heading for everything he writes.

## KEEP A RECORD

The material being produced by your child, from those first scribbles that are attempts at writing letters of the alphabet on to complete words, will accumulate quickly. The best way to save this material for comparison with later work is to put it in a file folder or a large envelope. Be sure to date the work as it's filed away. Children are pleased and proud of their files, and it generates enthusiasm when they look back and see how much progress they are making week by week. You'll also be pleased, and it will give you comfort and reassurance that your child is really learning. Remember, don't be in a hurry.

## PROGRESS AND SELF-ACTIVATION

Virtually all children will learn the alphabetic principle eventually, but don't look for a rapid response to this idea of sound-symbol relationships and how to make a word by putting those sounds together in the same order they came out of the mouth. It simply won't be completely absorbed in the first three, five, nine, seventeen, or thirty-four days. This process takes twenty weeks in the schools using the computer and all the other materials involved in the program, including teachers who have been trained to use the Writing to Read System.

On the other hand, when a child begins to get the idea and becomes eager to do any of these activities by himself, the parent's role changes to one of observer—much less of the co-worker or co-learner than was initially the case. What you need to establish is an atmosphere where you as parent

can continue to recede from a teacher's role to a joint-par-
ticipation role and then to a happy-observer role. There is
no way to know how long this will take. But after you get
a feel for the program and for your child's rate of progress,
you will sense the proper time to become the observer-guide.

## MORE VOCABULARY BUILDERS

The following series of activities is designed to increase
your child's recognition vocabulary, improve speaking competence, and increase his or her security with sounds, letters, and words. Since the importance of providing
opportunities for your child's language development can't
be overemphasized, we suggest that you:

- Arrange learning situations that suit your child's
  needs and wishes
- Use speech; take the time to foster curiosity and
  interest through talking together and listening
- Encourage your child to listen
- Answer questions in as much detail as you can
- Allow the time to follow each learning experience as far as the child's interest takes him
- Make the most of every situation by turning it
  into a learning opportunity, yet try to avoid
  stretching this concept too far by trying to turn
  perfectly simple activities into something fraught
  with meaning and learning
- Remember, if it can't be done with joy, don't do
  it; if the pleasure stops, stop.

## TRIPS

Children are always interested in going places and seeing
things. This applies to a trip to the supermarket as well as
a trip to Grandma's house or a vacation trip. Wherever you
go, you can encourage your child's speech and language

development. In the supermarket, at the fire station, the post office, the drugstore, the airport—you have the chance to name things and have your child name them. When you get home you can use the trip to stimulate the writing of words and the drawing of pictures and maps. A picture of the airport reveals planes and buildings, cars, buses and trucks, people, luggage, and all sorts of other items of interest. Words can be written on the elements of the picture—*jet, pilot, wing, tail, gas truck, ticket;* the list goes on and on.

Each trip, whether with the whole family or you alone with your child, offers equally valuable experiences. Picture-drawing and labeling the parts of the picture help to emphasize those experiences. This can all be done in an informal manner in addition to all of the other activities of the program.

## DRAMATIC PLAY

Play is a young child's work, and dramatic play in general is good for children. This kind of play, which often involves fantasy and make-believe, flows freely and involves changing roles and spontaneous action and response. Two games children love to play are House and Store. For these games any large cardboard carton will do. It makes a house, a cave, a tent, a spaceship, a candy store. Putting names on the parts—*window, door, motor, rope, shelf, rock*—and playing the roles of the people in these places enhances verbal and sight vocabulary.

The game of Store can take place in your own kitchen, and the shelves of your cabinets can become the shelves of the grocery. Playing with money and making change is a useful element here because it brings numbers and the concept of greater and lesser into play.

Of course, throughout all these situations the idea is to talk, to encourage the child to talk, to use old words and new ones, to form sentences and paragraphs, to make up stories with a beginning, a middle, and an end.

## COOKING

Cooking with your child is playing for real. Involve your child in the preparation of simple recipes that help reinforce the ideas of "how much" and the sequencing of events—first, second, next—as well as introducing a whole new vocabulary. The ingredients in a recipe represent new words, and the terms used in cooking—*boiling, pouring, shaking, spreading, patting, peeling, cutting, dicing, grating, baking, frying, mixing, mashing, stirring*—are all important in vocabulary building. If you use cookbooks that have pictures of various ingredients and pictures of the finished dishes themselves, they can be used for labeling purposes.

## THE GRAB BAG

Your child will be happy to say the names of things with you and for you if the process involves doing things he likes to do—for example, opening and closing a zipper, taking things out of a container, and putting things in a row. You can use an old purse for this game, or if you don't have that type of bag, a big shopping bag from the grocerystore will do. Fill it with a collection of small articles taken from various parts of the house including your child's toy box.

Have your child reach in and touch an object and identify it using the sense of touch alone and without taking it from the bag. When all the items have been felt and identified or guessed at, empty the bag and put each item back inside one at a time while naming each object as it is replaced. Later you can write down the words that identify those items, or help your child write them, and you can draw pictures of the items.

## SEQUENCING

This is a model of a language game that can be the basis for a great variety of "acting" stories that you and your

child can make up. All you do is read a sentence and wait
while your child acts out the instructions or the suggestions.
Here are some typical sentences:

- Brush your teeth.
- Button your shirt.
- Comb your hair.
- Walk to the bus.
- Get on the bus.
- Pay the driver.
- Get off the bus.
- Go to the store.
- Buy a present.
- Pay for the present.
- Get on the bus.
- Get off the bus and walk home.
- Open the door and go in.
- Wrap the present.
- Give the present to your mother.
- Wish her a Happy Birthday.

This is similar to charades (see opposite page), except
here you make the acting suggestions.


## TAPE RECORDING

Most folk tunes, nursery songs, and rounds have
straightforward melodies and are easy to learn. Use a tape
recorder and sing some of these familiar songs with your
child. Good melodies to sing include "Row, Row, Row Your
Boat," "Old MacDonald," and "Three Blind Mice." You can
add songs with verses that tell a story and songs that continue to add a line with each verse. Children delight in
playing these recordings back so they can hear and be sur-
prised by the sound of their own voice. They frequently learn
to sing the songs through happy repetition.

Of course, the recorder can also be used for playing

prerecorded tapes of children's songs but be sure that the words on these tapes are pronounced clearly since these words will help build vocabulary. Slurred words or the awkward sentence structure that is sometimes necessary for rhyming can be confusing. You may also want to use the recorder while you and your child talk in normal, everyday conversations. Playing these tapes can be fun as well as instructive because, again, sentence structure (or the lack of it) will be evident. This use of the recorder is valid as long as it doesn't become an intrusive element between the two of you. Like adults, some children are intimidated by the machine and become uncharacteristically quiet. You will quickly notice this if it occurs. If this happens, don't hesitate to put the machine aside because it is a valuable tool and you don't want to blunt its effective use in the future with a negative experience.

## CHARADES

Charades is a popular pantomime game that works in two ways. You can do things and ask your child to tell you what you are doing, and he or she can do things and ask you to identify them. Some things to try are washing hands, tying shoes, shaving, reading, writing, cooking, crying, chewing gum, eating popcorn, drinking from a glass, buttering bread, eating ice cream, and virtually any other action you think is appropriate.

## BODY LANGUAGE: A VARIATION ON CHARADES

All children use a great deal of body language, and there is a tendency for them to use more in households that are full of the noise from the television set, the radio, and stereo systems. In this kind of atmosphere human speech may be squelched. Children who grow up in a noisy atmosphere with little speech tend to use their bodies to express speech without words—their shoulders, hips, hands, fingers, faces, general posture—are all very expressive. One type of movement may indicate approval, another one disapproval, another withdrawal or fright. Parents learn to recognize these movements, many of which are done unconsciously, and they become ingrained methods of communication. Only when they are done to excess as a constant substitute for speech need we be concerned.

But we all use body language to a certain extent and this game takes advantage of the fact. We can and do use our face, hands, and body to express emotions and we use our bodies to emphasize what we say and how we feel as a normal practice. Either you or your child can try or you can take turns identifying the meaning of the following gestures by saying aloud what they mean:

| GESTURE | SAY |
| --- | --- |
| Crook your finger toward you | Come here |
| Turn up the corners of your mouth | Happy |
| Turn down the corners of your mouth | Sad |
| Move hands on imaginary piano | Playing the piano |
| Shake head from side to side | No |
| Shake head up and down | Yes |
| Scratching head | I don't know |
| Finger on lips | Quiet |
| Hands held far apart | Big |
| Hands held close | Small |
| Cradle your arms | Baby |
| Open hand, palm out | Stop |
| Point finger toward yourself | Me |
| Point finger at other person | You |
| Wave | Good-bye |

## WHAT RHYMES WITH _____?

Ask your child to think of a word that rhymes with the word you say, giving a little clue: for example, "What rhymes with *bake* that is something to eat?" The answer, of course, is cake. Here are some other examples:

- What rhymes with *mouse* and we live in one?
- What rhymes with *mile* and you do it when you're glad?
- What rhymes with *block* and you use it to tell time?
- What rhymes with *spool* and is a place where children go to learn?
- What rhymes with *moon* and you eat with it?
- What rhymes with *goat* and you wear it in the winter?
- What rhymes with *plow* and is an animal that gives milk?

You can move on from this by suggesting pairs of words and asking your child to make up sentence clues. For example:

| | |
|---|---|
| dish and fish | bark and spark |
| bed and red | sun and fun |
| wig and pig | water and daughter |
| clown and brown | slap and trap |
| sweet and street | egg and beg |
| rest and nest | sound and round |
| play and hay | grape and tape |
| look and book | cream and dream |
| bat and cat | goat and note |
| can and man | chair and scare |
| door and floor | book and look |
| hand and band | pen and hen |

There are unlimited possibilities here, and you will have no trouble thinking of many additional examples of your own.

## STORYTELLING

Being told stories may be more appealing to children than hearing them read because they can see your eyes, your mouth, and the gestures that help bring the story to life. Telling a story is not always easy, however. First you need the idea. Then you need to be able to tell it. To tell an effective story:

- Think of a story as a series of mental pictures, not memorized lines
- Use your voice, gestures, and timing effectively without being overly dramatic
- Speak clearly, vary the tone and quality of your voice, and try to make the voices of the characters in your story distinctive

The stories you choose to tell may be those you liked as a child, adventure tales, events that occurred in your family's past, or stories from real life. Stories of your experiences are of great interest to children, who find it hard to believe that you were once a child just like they are. If you tell the same story often enough and it is especially appealing to your child, eventually you can both sit down and write it out so your child can follow it word for word.

After a while your child will want to start telling stories of his own. They may be about friends, about a special event, about a trip to the store, or just a fantasy. These need not be long, involved stories, because the idea is to talk, to have an exchange between parent and child.

These suggestions are only representative of the kinds of things you can do with your child to enhance vocabulary development and encourage verbal and nonverbal communication. We suggest that you try some of these and then vary them for your particular needs and interests. Feel free to change these ideas, taking what you want and recombining them in other forms. We know that these activities work because we have tried them in homes and in the classroom. We also know from practical experience that they work at home and they accomplish what they are designed to do—lead to writing.

# CHAPTER 13

# THE WRITING EXERCISES

AS YOU'LL RECALL from our descriptions in earlier chapters, writing evolved through a long series of developmental stages, the first of which was oral language, using complex sounds to represent words. This was followed by the use of pictorial representations and decorative drawings painted on walls by cave dwellers who wanted to tell a story. This method of written communication slowly changed into a language of pictures or abstract symbolic representations that were used for the written words of a particular language. The hieroglyphics of the Egyptians, the ideograms of the Chinese, and the picture writing of the American Indians are examples of this form of written communication. The next and final step in this evolution was the development of the alphabet. As we know it in English today, it is a series of twenty-six letters, or sound-symbols, that are assembled and reassembled in thousands and thousands of combinations to make words.

If your child has been following the program we have laid out, he will eventually have progressed through all of these developmental stages:

- He has been encouraged to talk and listen
- He has represented his ideas by drawing and labeling pictures
- He has used symbols and alphabet letters
- He has begun to use the phonemic writing system, the alphabet symbols, to represent his speech on paper.

Writing to Read nurtures the connection between the processes of language—speaking, listening, writing, and reading. What we're striving for is the development of writing skills, and we have been working to set the stage for this because children learn to write by:

- Hearing their own speech sounds
- Associating those sounds with the letters of the alphabet
- Sequencing speech sounds and print symbols
- Writing those sequenced speech symbols in the form of words.

Now that the stage has been fully set, we want to take that next step from sequencing speech symbols in the form of words and begin sequencing those words into sentences and stories. These sentences and finally the stories told by several sentences can be reproduced on paper with a pencil or other writing tool or on the typewriter.

It should be stressed here that all writing is rewriting. Writing is editing. At the same time that we're expounding the doctrine that writing is the beginning stage of learning to read, we believe that proficiency in writing is a function of rewriting. In the process of writing your child will make errors, errors that he recognizes as he puts the word on paper. The procedure we recommend for editing is the crossing out of that mistake, whether it's a word or a letter or an entire line. Children do this instinctively as they are learning and there is absolutely nothing wrong with the practice. Children don't yet have the motor skills to write precisely, and whatever level of skill they do have is sorely tested when they are involved in a thinking process that is a difficult task in itself. It takes thought to construct a word, and in the process of thinking we have false starts, we make errors, and we correct errors.

NOTE: The writing suggestions in this chapter may appear to be part of a linear progression—that is, "Now that the other things have been learned we are moving on to the writing stage." This isn't the case. As we have said many times, many of the activities in this program may take place concurrently. Though it is possible that you are just beginning the actual writing phase of your work, it is more likely that many of these kinds of activities have already occurred. Any and all of these suggestions are designed to be ongoing with the word games, the storytelling, the work with clay, slate and chalk, the sand tray, and all the rest. Progress is like a walking pendulum. Children learn and then they seem to forget. Then they learn the same thing over again through another activity or with different materials. Then they may forget again and again, even as we did. But they learn a little bit more each time.

## STEP ONE—WRITING PHONEME PRACTICE WORDS

If you have not begun the practice of having your child write words, you should start now because the child is ready and so are you. In Writing to Read we use the words from the ten computer cycles for these writing exercises. We don't know what words you have used and are using to represent and teach the forty-two phonemes, but we recommend that you use the words from the computer cycles for this next stage as follows:

1. cat, dog, fish
2. pig, sun, bed
3. rabbit, leg, three (rabit, thrē)
4. man, snake, vase (snāk, vās)
5. jump, hand, wagon
6. yard, moon, kite (kīt)
7. zipper, straw, smoke (ziper, smōk)
8. turtle, chair, house (turtl, hous)
9. oil, horse, wheel (hors, whēl)
10. uniform, book, butter (ūniform, buter)

```
     a  b  c  d  e  f  g  h  i  j  k  l  m
  a                                           au-aw
  e                                           ar
  i                                           er
  o                                           oo
  u                                           or
  ch                                          oi
  sh                                          ur
  th                                          air
  wh
     n  o  p  q  r  s  t  u  v  w  x  y  z
```

These are the phonemes needed to write all the sounds a child can hear when speaking English. They are written in 500 different ways in ordinary spelling. Writing them this way at the beginning keeps the problem within the understanding of most children. They will, of course, write many words in strange ways. Encourage them to write and they will eventually write and spell better than other children.

Have your child write one of the phoneme words at a time, keeping in mind what we just said about correcting errors. These words should first be written by hand and then typed. After a word has been written, ask your child to read the word. When this idea has been grasped—and it won't take more than one or two days—use the same words and begin to write two and then three words at a time, but try to make sure that there is only one word to each line. Follow the same procedure of writing the word, then reading the word, writing the word, then reading the word.

Of course, we recommend using a typewriter for all of these exercises. If you do use a typewriter, use half-sheets of paper for these word lists and have your child type his name and the date at the top of each sheet when he can.

Save the handwritten and typed examples and put them in your child's file.

## STEP TWO—WRITING NEW WORDS

You have been working on forming new words in a variety of ways. You have used storytelling, matching alphabet letters to words that describe an animal or a household object or an ingredient in a recipe, charades, and other word games. Now, write the letters of the phonemic alphabet across a sheet of paper for reference and have your child make new words from those letters. This can be done at any stage of the learning process. For example, at the end of two or three weeks you may have worked on only the following phonemes (derived from *cat, dog, fish, pig, sun,* and *bed*):

```
        a  b  c  d  e  f  g    i
   sh
        n  o  p        s  t  u
```

There are plenty of opportunities in these phonemes to form new words. *Tag, fit, dig, fig,* and *fish* are good examples. If your child has difficulty forming words by simply looking at the letters (and this is entirely possible), then you can help the process along by giving a description, a sort of definition of the word. For example:

- What swims in the water?
- How do you make a hole in the ground?
- If we are playing a game and I _____ you, then you're it.
- What is something to eat that rhymes with *pig?*
- When we go to buy shoes, I always ask if the shoes_____ on your feet.

Tutor your child by pronouncing the sound of each letter in the new word. Follow the same procedure as you did in step one, writing the word (one on each line), reading the word, typing the word, reading the word again. Repeat the exercise as many times as you want or think necessary. Of course, as more phonemes are added to your list, the potential for forming new words continues to grow.

## STEP THREE—SENTENCE WRITING

The next level of writing is sentence writing. This process of putting words together in logical and sensible order seems quite natural to adults, but it is a good deal more complicated for children than writing individual words. You have been reading to your child and talking in sentences for some time, so the idea of words in a row is not a new one; the practice, however, is new. To bridge this gap help the process along by pointing out the way words in books, newspapers, and magazines are separated by a space and are printed on a straight line. Explain how a sentence begins with a capital letter and usually ends with a period and that the words between those two "keys" are called a sentence. Further explain that there needs to be a space between words when they are written by hand and when they are typed on the typewriter so they will be easier to read and understand. Then show your child how to use the space bar of the typewriter to separate the words in a sentence and how to write several words on one line as it is done in books. Here you may have to help for a while, but don't be concerned if there is more than one space between words, only that there is at least one.

Not all children are able to write sentences or phrases immediately, and some people use what are called "sentence starters" to overcome this initial reticence. These phrases are supposed to encourage a child to begin sentence writing and to eventually encourage storytelling. There are mixed opinions on the use of this type of assistance. We don't stand flatly on one side of the issue or the other. If you have a child full of words, stories, and enthusiasm for telling you something, then sentence starters are an imposition and an artificial constraint on such a child. If, at the other end of the scale, you have a very silent child whose normal speech is limited to single words, the creation of a sentence is going to take considerable stimulus.

The first child will need no prodding and will rather quickly write sentences like these:

> Wun day my bruther went to the county jail for a field trip.

> On friday my granma and granpa will kum.

> I wood put it in the fregerrator and let it freez for three ouers and thin take it out.

The second child will need some help but will soon get the idea if you can start with a picture as a stimulus—an animal, a spaceship, a baseball player, a piano, whatever you choose—and say such things as:

- What does this picture make you think of?
- Tell me something about this picture.
- Who (or what) do you think this is?
- Does this picture make you happy or sad?

Another way to stimulate sentence writing is to provide the first few words of the sentence. This can be done based on a picture taken from a book or magazine or simply by saying the first few words. Here are a few ideas:

- My sister is . . .
- I wish . . .
- Tomorrow . . .
- Yesterday . . .
- When I grow up . . .
- My favorite . . .
- Spinach is . . .
- I think . . .
- If . . .
- The last time . . .
- The next time . . .
- I am going . . .

- I went . . .
- Why do . . .
- My mother . . .
- My brother . . .

As your child begins to show some facility for assembling a sentence, you can help the process along with a series of what we call "I like" sentences. Each sentence begins with the words "I like . . ." and is filled in by words that represent things in the child's life, such as animals, toys, and people. As we've said, children's humor consists, in part, of the juxtaposition of things that don't fit together and the I Like game lends itself readily to humor. For example, you can make word cards that read *daddy, mother, grandma, sister,* and so forth, and then some incongruous things such as *snakes, bugs, dirt, thunder,* and others. The child writes "I like" and then you flash a card and the child writes the word. Clearly some will come out funny and this is appreciated by most children.

Another cooperative way to stimulate sentence writing is the alternating sentence game. You can begin by saying something and writing it down or typing it. Then your child responds by saying something and writing or typing it. These kinds of games often work best when what is said is funny or silly. For example:

PARENT:  I have a blue face.
CHILD:   A blue face is ugly.
PARENT:  I need to make my face another color.
CHILD:   I have an idea. I'll make it red.
PARENT:  That's much better now.
CHILD:   Yes, I like this red color.
PARENT:  Oh, no. It's not so good after all.
CHILD:   When you look real close, it's funny.
PARENT:  Maybe blue was all right after all.

An extension of this story-making idea is one that many educators agree encourages sentence and story writing. You begin by encouraging your child to tell a story, and while he or she is talking, you record it like a stenographer by

writing the words in large letters on paper. Some children
will respond to this idea with a flow of words that come
faster than you can write them down. If your child is very
loquacious, you may want to use a tape recorder instead of
paper because it's easier, though it won't produce the same
record of words on paper. Play it back in very short phrases.
Then write them. Others will have to be encouraged to begin
and then, once started, to continue. In the first instance you
may have to ask the child to slow down, and in the second
case you will have to cajole and lead. In either situation,
don't worry. The talkative child will not be upset if some of
the words aren't on the paper. The reticent child will eventually loosen up and the flow will come. Again, keep in mind
that children differ. Some are quiet and some are vocal, and
you should handle your child as you see fit. A child who has
difficulty verbally composing a four-word sentence can be
encouraged with such terms as the following:

- What happened next?
- Really, tell me more.
- What did he say then?
- What did you like about it?
- What didn't you like about it?
- Did it scare you?
- Did it make you laugh?

Even those children who need little incentive to write
sentences sometimes get stuck. All that need be done in
most cases is to suggest topics that can help get them on
the track: television, comics, sports, food, friends, brothers
and sisters, grandparents, vacations, toys, games, books,
music.

One of our favorite techniques for stimulating sentence
writing is the game called rebus writing. Rebus writing
preceded the alphabet. You probably know it as a series of
letters and pictures that form a sentence. A rebus is really
a pictorial pun that represents a word, a phrase, or a sentence with symbols, pictures, parts of words, and numbers.
For example, the rebus for the preposition *for* is *4*; a picture
of the eye is the rebus for *I*; a picture of the eye and a tin

can and a stick figure of a person walking is the rebus *I can walk*. Children delight in this game and it's a good solid progression in the process of learning to write.

I ate carrots and corn

Rebus games and drawing pictures to illustrate sentences enhance and underscore the learning process that is taking place, and that's why we encourage children to make drawings that further explain their sentences and stories.

To ensure that all the words being written during these work sessions are being learned, you should ask your child to read to you what he or she has written during that period. If there are words that are not remembered, you can help and then suggest that they be tried again the next day.

Of course, all writing need not be done in a formal manner. Children greatly enjoy projects that require them to write for real reasons. Two popular ideas are grocery lists ("What I would like to eat") and short notes (from two words to several sentences) addressed to another member of the family and stuck to the refrigerator.

## STEP FOUR—SIMPLE STORY WRITING

The progression from writing sentences to writing stories is a logical and basically simple one. A child need only understand that a story is composed of several sentences about the same subject, and that those sentences should be written just the way they are in the stories he or she has been hearing from books—with the idea that each story has a beginning, a middle, and an end. You can explain this further by talking about any book that has been read and by pointing out that stories move from one step to another. Using "Jack and the Beanstalk" as an example, you can explain how in the beginning Jack went to the market, and that the next thing he did was sell the cow for a bag of beans. Next he went home and his mother got angry and threw the beans out. Then the beanstalk grew and he climbed it and found the giant's castle and so forth. As we've said, most children understand that things happen in an orderly way, so they don't require any more help than your repetition of one of their favorite phrases: "And then what happened?"

A child's first efforts will be appropriately simple:

Clifford is a dog.
Clifford is mī frnd.
Clifford līks mē.
Clifford lks bōns.

One day I met Jeremy and Mrs. Brown. We had fun. We had cholcot pī. It was good.

I wish I had a rabbit. I would feed him carrots.

Such stories need be no longer than two to four sentences in length, but even writing of that length can convey a sense of imagination, drama, time, and place. Writing those first stories isn't always easy. Many children have more ideas than they can possibly get down on paper. It is different for us adults, who write words rather automatically, to understand how much thinking a child is doing in constructing each word a letter or two at a time to represent each sound in that word. It is hard and exciting work. Enjoy the product with them.

Some children have difficulty thinking of topics for their stories just as they did for sentences. So if a child asks for help at the beginning of or during the story-writing process, feel free to offer suggestions and guidance but don't write the story for him. The sources of story ideas are everywhere. Pictures and drawings clipped from newspapers and magazines are good sources of inspiration, as are television, radio, and music. A picture of an airplane and a few questions from a parent ("Where do you think the airplane is going?" or "Would you like to take a trip?") are usually enough to stimulate a child's creative juices.

As in all cases with children's writing, the parent should read the work carefully and make appropriate comments. Those comments, however, should only be offered in a positive sense, always avoiding any criticism of the subject matter, spelling, or grammar, because these elements are unimportant at this stage of skill development and negative criticism can be destructive rather than constructive.

After you have read your child's story, you can and should encourage additions by asking questions:

- Can you tell me more about this Mr. Jones?
- What time of the year did this happen?
- Can you tell me what happened next?
- This is a sad ending. Can you think of a happy ending?
- This is a happy ending. Can you think of a sad ending?

A good method of stimulating story writing is to use the word cards that you have made for other activities—for example, the words you used when you were working in the kitchen with the recipe game. These words can be placed in a sequence on the table by your child and then a story can be written using them. All the directions in a recipe are useful words for writing and sequencing. What is desirable is a clear piece of writing, not the recipe itself. "Now is the time to beat the eggs and now is the time to put the eggs in the mix" represents a sequence of acts that is real, and it is useful to write them and verbalize them. Here are three recipes written by kindergarten children in the Writing to Read program in Raleigh, North Carolina:

Spegeti
*10 unyuns*
*3 cups of peper*
*10 cups ful of salt*
*2 spoons of venger*
*10 noodles*
*50 cups of woter*

*Mix everthing up with the woter. Kook on top of the stov at 5 degres timter. Kook for 5 minutes. Drink pepsi with this.*

Piza
*A littl bit of chez*
*1 pakag of sawsag*
*Some red stuf for the botum*
*A lot of piza shels*

*Put the red stuf on the botum of the Piza shels. Put the chez on next. Then put the sawsag on the top of everething. Put it in the uvn at 2 degres. Kook for 2 minits.*

Yogurt
*Fiftin strawberees*
*1 cup full of cream*
*A spoon full of apple joose*
*A spoon full of sugar*

*I wood micks all of it up. I wood put it in the fregerrator and let it freez for three ouers and thin take it out. And I wood let my Mama eat it. She wood drink orange joose with it.*

This kind of writing can be created with anywhere from six to fifteen word cards. This exercises a child's capacity to recognize the word itself or the hieroglyph of the word—

that is, the total configuration or profile of the word—to sequence the word and to get the idea across.

Story starters are useful at this stage of a child's writing development and story enders are equally as good. Endings like the following can also be good story starters:

- . . . but next summer it will be different.
- . . . and then I woke up.
- . . . sometimes you learn things the hard way.
- . . . and that was the last time I saw him.
- . . . was the most exciting game of the year.
- . . . my best birthday ever.
- . . . and I have loved it ever since.
- . . . and I'll never do that again.
- . . . is now my best friend.
- . . . was very scary.
- . . . I promise.

## STEP FIVE—INTERMEDIATE STORY WRITING

At this stage of a child's writing development there is less and less need for parental suggestion on subject matter and more and more reliance on the imagination and resourcefulness of the child. What we mean by "more advanced" here is the development of stories that:

- Use more words
- Use more and more new words
- Contain sentences that are in more logical sequence
- Contain longer sentences
- Use fewer connectors like *and* and *then* and *because*
- Have some description
- Have a starting point and a conclusion.

You may still have to offer some hints or story ideas, but suggestions that are more abstract can now be used.

Instead of just using a picture (which is perfectly fine), you can ask a child to write about:

- A special event like a birthday
- A story that you have read to him
- How he feels about something or someone
- Something that is purely imaginary.

You'll soon be seeing stories like this one:


My ferst bābē doll

one day mī mommy wōk me up and I got drest and I āt brafist mī mommy took mē to thus toī stor and I had ten dolers and I bot a bābē doll it wuz five dolers and with thu rest uv mī munē I got a pak uv stikers and with thu rest uv mī munē I bot a stiker ablm and thn wē went home and wē āt luch and after then I went out side for a kupl auwers then I kām in and āt diner. thu end.


As always, these stories are written by hand, then read, then typed, then read again. At this stage, too, it is a good idea to encourage some editing, some changing after the fact. Explain that this doesn't mean anything is wrong, only that it may be possible to say something in a different way or to say it better or to find another word that means the same thing. It's also a good time to start going back over work to check the clarity of the phonemic spelling and make sure that the child is satisfied with the way all the words look and read. Correct spelling must not be an issue. If you choose to make it a problem at this stage, you will dry up their joy in writing. Your child will begin to notice those discrepancies between "correct" spelling and phonemic spelling—for example, the single most common word in English is the article *the*. It may be written the way it sounds, "thu," in early efforts and changed by most children to "the" very quickly.

## STAGE SIX—ADVANCED STORY WRITING

When your child reaches this stage of writing proficiency, your job is not to encourage writing—because that will take care of itself—but to find ways to continue to expand your child's thinking and story-line development through your expressed pleasure and the applause of everyone in the family. The following questions can help this process when preceded by "That's a great story":

- What happened before your story started?
- What happened after your story ended?
- Tell me more about this person or what happened.

The following, by a student in Florida, is a good example of advanced story writing:

### Bubbles by Lori*

One day I was walking along the fents and I saw some Bubbles.
So I climed up the fents to see what was making the Bubbles.
A man was selling Bubbles! So I bought myself some Bubbles.
I started to blō by the tree! I bloo out a Kangroo and all sorts of things.
I bloo a boot and an airplane and I started to blow a snake.
And I did make a snake and I stared at him and he almost ate me.
But! I started to make a cat to scare him away and the cat scared me away.
But I made an elafant to scare the cat away and the elafant scared me.

---

*Each of these lines was a caption for a full-page picture drawn by Lori.

So I made a mouse to scare him away.
But they floo away and I popt them.
An I pord out the Bubbles.
There was no more but a Dragon.

In essence this allows your child to become an "author," to expand his vocabulary, to stimulate interest in language and writing, and to spur his imagination. At this stage children can also begin to make their own picture books of stories, as Lori did in the one above, by adding a part each day until they have a sheaf of papers that can be put together in a notebook or bound in a folder with special illustrated covers.

## THE PERSONAL DICTIONARY

We suggest that children begin to keep a personal dictionary the very first time they encounter a new word that they have trouble remembering. The dictionary helps them remember these new words and it also stimulates them to actively search out new words to write. You and your child can make a notebook of twenty-six pages (using heavy paper or oaktag for the cover), one folded sheet for each letter of the alphabet stapled or clipped together, with a 1-inch lowercase letter at the top of each page. As the child learns new words, those words should be entered on the appropriately designated alphabet page. This kind of record saves time in checking the spelling of new words and provides practice in alphabetizing skills and associating words with their beginning sounds.

## ONE MORE REMINDER ON CORRECTING

I can't emphasize often enough that parents must try to restrain the impulse to correct their children. Growth in early learning is better accomplished by fertilizing a child's competency than by pruning a child's errors. I use the analogy of a growing plant and it isn't farfetched. A child's growth is fertilized when attention is called to things the child does well. We know when something is done correctly and well, but a child may not be conscious of how good something is. When a parent says, "Look how well you've made an *a*," or "That is a very good picture of a face," or "You did those cards very well today," or "Your story is very good," it's critically important to a child. On the other hand, nothing positive is accomplished by saying, "That's not a very good letter *c*," or "Write that sentence again and make it better," or "Your story doesn't make any sense." The way to subtly handle the job of correction is to say, "I can't see a letter *c*," or "I don't know what that word is. You tell me. Say it again." If the child says that is, indeed, a letter *c* or indicates that the word is clear to him, then go on from there and leave the situation alone. "Accent the positive" is an old and good adage and it's fundamentally sound for little children.

Of course, we feel it's also necessary to give praise without being artificial or dripping sugar on the child with over-praise. Reserve your praise for what deserves it, and what deserves it is progress, the adequacy or skill with which the child does something. Acknowledge each new accomplishment and speak your pride. Keep in mind that within any piece of work there are some good elements. Speak about those and your child will grow.

## SOME OTHER REMINDERS

**One:** The reason for the large number of activities provided here (and there are many more you can devise on your own) is that some of them may not be appropriate for your child for a variety of reasons or at a particular time, and you may not be comfortable with others. Charades is a good example. Many parents are less comfortable with panto-miming ideas than their children. Don't feel chagrined about this because there are many people who can't do charades or sing a song or make up an imaginary story. Remember there are some things others can't do that you can do well. If you feel unqualified for an activity or uncomfortable with it, there is no reason to pressure yourself. Some of them are less appropriate for you than others; your child will not be comfortable, nor will you, with every activity. When this happens, drop it. We said earlier that one of the criteria for a good learning situation is that *both* the parent and the child feel comfortable and are able to have a good time doing the activity together.

**Two:** Whatever activity you choose for the day should be the only activity for that day. All of these activities reinforce each other and should be taken in due time. Don't press to get many things into one time period.

**Three:** Set a special time aside for these activities every day. Try not to let anything interfere with this special time.

**Four:** I don't think we can repeat enough that parents should not push their children. Don't be in a hurry. Learning will not happen faster.

**Five:** We have been following this path throughout Writing to Read:

- Your child is learning to read by learning to write.
- This is happening because he is learning the symbols for writing by learning that the symbols are letters that stand for the sounds in words.
- He is learning that speaking is the prelude to this and listening to speech is a parallel accompaniment.
- All of these things have been going on in all the things that we have suggested.

In Writing to Read we try not to separate formally the teaching of reading, writing, talking, and listening. Children are doing all of these things when they learn to write. They think; they talk; they listen to the sounds in the words; they write those sounds to make those words; and they read what they have written. Each step is connected to the next step and the logic of it helps children learn.

## THE TRANSITION TO STANDARD SPELLING

The phonemic spelling system you have taught your child is designed to make it easier for him to put down on paper the sounds he makes when he speaks. We know that, using our system, quite often a child's spelling will not correspond to standard spelling for about half the words in the English language.

Our experience has proved that this will not be a concern for long. Many children seem to know how to spell some words correctly without any difficulty from the very first day, writing words the way they remember having seen them in books, on labels, on signs, on television, and elsewhere. Those children with difficulty in making the change will make it as they develop phonemic spelling proficiency.

If you try to hurry this process, you run the risk of inhibiting a child's progress in writing, because they will begin to choose safe words for their sentences and stories, words they know for certain in their visual memory, while avoiding the many more-interesting words they have in their speaking vocabularies.

As children read, however, they discover on their own that there are standardized spellings for words, and they notice the inconsistencies* between the way they are spelling and the correct way. So it really isn't necessary to teach correct spelling. It happens naturally.

---

*Enjoy with your child the humor in the historical irregularities in standard spelling. For example, say these out loud:

1. *Too, to, two, women.* Shouldn't it be called "oo-men" and how about *who?*
2. *Rough* and *cuff.*
3. *Through* and *threw.*
4. *Hair* and *tear* and then *hear.*
5. *Bear* and *bare.*
6. *Ouch* and *touch* and *much.*

Looking for words that can be written in many different ways will help your child to understand that learning to spell is something that they just have to do even when "it doesn't make sense."

# CHAPTER 14

# HOW TO ASSESS PROGRESS

I like Mrs. Calhoun becaus she has tawt me how to rēd and wrīt this year in kindergarten on the ComPuter. I can wrīt a storey and TyPe it and rēd it to you. It makes me happy becaus I do not haft to ask my bruther to tell me the werds. We go to the conputer room everē day. Mrs. Calhoun is my fāvert techer.

EVERY PARENT WANTS to know if, and how much, their child is learning, and you will certainly want to know if Writing to Read is working with your child. There are three areas to which you can apply various yardsticks that will give you an idea of progress. All of these are indicative but none is perfect, and you certainly should make no long-term judgments about your child's ability to learn based on these criteria. Besides, to a large degree you will have to rely on your personal, though probably not very objective, evaluations in measuring your own child's progress in writing, spelling, and reading.

## EVALUATING YOUR CHILD'S WRITING

Here are two questions you will want to ask yourself:

- What does good writing look and sound like?
- How do I know if real progress is being made?

These are valid and legitimate questions. Unfortunately they can't be answered precisely because there are no standardized tests of "good writing." Still, we wanted to get some answers to these questions, since for any evaluation to be useful it needs valid and reliable measures. As part of their overall evaluation of the Writing to Read System, the Educational Testing Service devised a method of assessing student writing. To compile their data, they asked teachers of children in the program and others who were not in it to have their children write on a common topic for a half hour under standard and equal conditions. This test was given first before any classes had been exposed to Writing to Read.

The title selected for this writing test was "One Day I Found a Magic Hat," and as was to be expected, some children wrote well-developed essays and others wrote a few unintelligible phrases. The same test was later given to "graduates" of Writing to Read and to similar children in comparison schools who had not had the program. In all, about 5,000 writing samples were gathered.

These tests were scored by some fifty kindergarten and first grade teachers who were trained by ETS in a special process of rating children's writing. One of the problems, as defined by ETS at the outset (a problem you will have as a parent as well), was defining what good writing is for young children. In the end, it was determined that the essays would be judged primarily on the ideas they presented, the development and expression of those ideas, the way they were organized, on sentence structure, and fluency. Penmanship, spelling, and punctuation were not part of the criteria.

A large random sample of papers was reviewed and thirty papers were selected from the kindergarten level and another thirty from the first grade level. It was felt by the evaluators that these sixty papers represented the general range of writing ability of the students. Then specific features were identified that seemed to distinguish the "best" papers from the "next best" and so on in each grade. Six levels of quality were then designated, and they formed the basis for the six-point scale used in the scoring of the writing. Each writing sample was read by two readers and each gave a score of 1 to 6 to the sample.

So that you can better judge what all this means, here are some first grade writing samples as they were rated by score from lowest to highest:

*Score of 1*
One da I found a magic hat.
I wish I was on the moon.
I wish I had a car.
I wish I had a gardin.

*Score of 1*
One day I found a magic hat. Mi fren is name herman. he is a good fren. He has a cat.

*Score of 2*
One day I found a magic hat. I at jecrim and we floo. it gav me a 100 tows. And a dog and to rabbts. And then it turndt green and red then black. And then i wus roln. And then i wutht theat i had a clubhous. and then it made a car. and then it tot and tot. And this ol.

*Score of 2*
One day I found a magic hat If I found a magic hat I will get all the other hats and all the cars. If I found a magic hat I will go up the hill flying. If I had a magic hat I will go to the sky. I will get a bike from the store.

*Score of 3*
One day I found a magic hat. I wished that I could fly. I flue home. When I got hom I wished everything.

*Score of 3*
One day I found a magic hat Jody and Dana found a magic hat to so they will go to the moon. My mom wint to the mooves to.

*Score of 4*
One day I found a magic hat. I wished that I had
evrething in the world. One day I found some gold.
The next day in my groge I found a jet. My dad
allso was mad at me. The next day he was not. And
avry day somethim good wood hapin. My best wish
was the jet. This was after school. the hat was
black. Thas whet I liked about it.

*Score of 4*
One day I found a magic hat. on the way home from
school. I put it on and I wished I coud have all the
cash I want. My mother said no and I was sad.

*Score of 5*
One day I found a magic hat. I put it on and I could
do anything I wanted to. I could own a pizza shop.
I could live in a castle. But what I wanted the most
of all was a friend. So I weshed I had a friend and
I got one.

*Score of 5*
One day I found a magic hat. when I word it rit-
sidup it made a rabbit come out uf the hat with
tahe jumt and jumt arad. The rabbit lived in the
city. he cums in my bakyrd and ese the karit and
I love the rabbit. the rabbit dus tris.

*Score of 6*
One day I found a magic hat. It was black and
shiney. It looked like it was new. I was in the field
then. When I said airplane I turned into an airplane. Then the hat said, "hello." I was frightend.
The hat kept talking to me and tallking to me until
a green car drove by. The hat jumped right in. And
I never saw it again.

*Score of 6*
One day I found a magic hat. it said on it with this
hat you can do anything. So I put it on and wished

and then I began to fly! I sward thew the air but
then my hat fell of. I started to crash but then a
bird flew up and gave it to me! I flew faster and
faster and I went home. the next day a bully tried
to beat me up but I had my magic hat. He punched
me in the mouth but then his tooth came out! but
then a breeze came and lost my hat! then a car was
going to crash into me but then I woke up and found
I was only dreaming.

It may be helpful and reassuring to you to note your
child's progress through these successively mature levels of
writing. Please remember, however, that they are only representative of writing at ages four and five and are an imperfect guide, just as samples of various levels of adult writing
would be an imperfect method of judging writing ability.
Therefore, don't worry if your child's work doesn't resemble
any of these examples because it may still be a perfectly
good piece of work.

In addition to these samples, we have compiled the
following criteria, adapted from those used by ETS, for you
to use in judging your child's writing. They represent the
normal progress made by the children in learning to write
through the Writing to Read System.

You will recall that we started with children drawing
pictures which they then labeled. Writing these first words,
the words used to help children learn that letters stand for
the sounds inside words, is the first step.

The second step is a giant step mentally. We call it
"making words," that is constructing a new word out of the
letter-sounds a child has learned to use. Remember, the
Chinese civilization never got there. Only now is China
attempting to use an alphabet.

Step three in writing is the construction of the simplest sentences, frequently characterized by "I like _____,
I like _____, I like _____" in a list of mother, father, sister,
brother, ice cream, and a pet.

Step four comes with the growing confidence in the
ability to write "everything I can say!" These are the early

stories that have a three- to five-sentence continuity on a single topic.

Step five represents real growth in self-confidence and a sense of control over writing ideas and stories of some greater length.

Step six is a sophisticated story of internal interest with a logical progression to a reasoned or humorous conclusion. We have noted that some older six-year-olds with a language maturity that seems to be unusual will move toward nonfiction writing. They will precociously read children's encyclopedias in order to write realistically about the planets or flowers or bears in Alaska.

We fully understand that the distinctions at these various levels of writing skill are often minor, and we also know from experience that parents have difficulty in trying not to judge their own child's work. What is important is to note progress, not comparative status. You can make some evaluations of progress, and if you try hard to be objective, you can make use of these carefully developed criteria.

Again, let me stress that all children are different and they learn at different rates. Don't expect your child's work to be at the sixth level after a few months. That doesn't mean he or she is destined for failure in the world of written expression. What it probably means is that the child is perfectly normal in this area of cognition and will soon develop.

## EVALUATING YOUR CHILD'S READING

When a child reads what he has just written, he is using a different set of cognitive skills than he used when he encoded that written material in the first place. The presumption that a child learning to write can automatically read is a good one, but it isn't always accurate. As I listen to children reading what they have written, it is clear to me that a different mental function is involved. That difference—decoding rather than encoding—often results in children reading what they have just written with more difficulty than one would expect. But it is a temporary condition that improves with repeated practice.

How, then, do you know if your child is learning to read? For you at home, the answer is not complicated. You listen and you observe your child's growing desire to read silently.

The most common measurement used by schools is the standard reading test. A number of such tests are good and valid. The following were used by the school districts and were summarized by ETS as one element in their evaluation of the reading abilities of Writing to Read students:

- California Achievement Tests
- Stanford Early School Assessment Series
- Iowa Tests of Basic Skills
- Comprehensive Tests of Basic Skills
- Metropolitan Readiness Tests.

One or more of these tests is given regularly in schools throughout the country.

These tests are not available for home use, and even if they were, they aren't appropriate for that purpose. A parent doesn't want to sit down and administer a formal reading test to his or her child. There are, however, ways to measure reading skills that don't depend on a formal testing instrument.

Here are some of the preliminary skills to look for if your child is four years old or beginning kindergarten:

- Recognition of letter forms
- Recognition of letter names
- Recognition of letter sounds
- Matching sounds to letters and letter names
- Comprehension of oral information
- Recognition of some words
- Ease in speaking (evident language skill).

These are the first signs of learning to read. As a child gains skill, he or she will recognize more words, begin to read sentences, increase vocabulary, comprehend oral information more fully, and begin to analyze words. As children reach the first grade in school, after formal exposure to the Writing to Read System in kindergarten, the great majority will be able to:

- Read words
- Read sentences
- Comprehend these words and sentences
- Comprehend while listening
- Analyze words
- Orally express thoughts clearly
- Continually increase vocabulary
- Begin to spell correctly.

It is possible that these skills are even more difficult for a parent to judge than the writing skills we talked about above. As a parent, therefore, you have to use common sense in making these evaluations. It's probably not a good idea to sit with your child and try to test him against these standards, which will be more easily and more completely tested in the schools. As we noted with writing ability, if your child does not show strong reading skills at age five, he or she will probably still fall within the normal range of skill development. Remember that teaching children to read at age five is new to American schools, and there are many teachers and reading experts who believe it shouldn't be tried at all.

## EVALUATING YOUR CHILD'S SPELLING

While writing and reading are difficult skills to test in your child, spelling is easy. If a word is spelled correctly, we know it instantly. If it is spelled wrong, it is often easy to see why the error occurred and to correct the error. Don't forget, however, that we have been teaching a phonemic alphabet, and as we've warned, there will be discrepancies between your child's spelling and "book" spelling because of that fact.

As part of the ETS evaluation, a special study of spell-

ing skills was conducted to determine if Writing to Read
children were learning to spell correctly given the reliance
of the program on phonemic spelling. The results of those
ten-word tests showed that Writing to Read and non–Writing to Read children scored about equally, though Writing
to Read students did score slightly higher.

The tests were administered by the classroom teachers
who read the words to the children in short sentences and
then asked them to write the words on paper. The following
words and sentences were used for testing. The test word
is underlined.

For kindergarten children:
1. He is six <u>feet</u> tall.
2. We took a <u>ride</u> on the bus.
3. She <u>made</u> sandwiches for lunch.
4. The girl <u>was</u> tired.
5. I <u>cut</u> my finger.
6. Going to the circus was <u>fun</u>.
7. We saw a <u>big</u> dog.
8. I have a bike at <u>home</u>.
9. The boy said <u>yes</u>.
10. I can write my <u>name</u>.

[Please note that five of these words differ from
their phonemic spelling or contain a final silent *e*,
penalizing Writing to Read children who did not
make the change.]

For first graders:
1. He is six <u>feet</u> tall.
2. We took a <u>ride</u> on the bus.
3. Mary wishes she <u>could</u> swim.
4. Going to the circus was <u>fun</u>.
5. This is a <u>good</u> book.
6. <u>They</u> have a big car.
7. The bird is in the <u>tree</u>.
8. He did not say <u>anything</u>.
9. She is very <u>pretty</u>.
10. We went to the circus <u>together</u>.

[Again, five of these words differ in their phonemic spelling from their standard spelling, penalizing Writing to Read children.]

Despite these spelling differences in the test words, Writing to Read children did slightly better than children taught to spell conventionally. Please remember that premature insistence on correct spelling will tend to inhibit good writing for the rest of your child's life. Writing is rewriting. First drafts are efforts to use the best words and sentences we can bring to the surface of our minds and put on paper. The habit, taught in childhood, of rejecting the best expression we can devise because of a fear of misspelling produces a fundamental reluctance to write. So while as a nation we grow alarmed when we learn that 27 million adults cannot read the English language, we should be equally concerned that the inability to write a coherent paragraph is evidenced even among our high school graduates. The blighting effect of correcting children's early spelling lasts a lifetime.

## A LAST WORD ON JUDGING PROGRESS

No test, either objective or subjective, gives an accurate measure of learning development. IQ tests, long thought to be a measure of brain capacity, are now known to be limited measures of limited usefulness. You are the best judge of your child's progress. You know your child's strengths and weaknesses. Rely on your judgment and the knowledge that all normal children will learn the skills of writing, reading, and spelling. It is, for most, simply a matter of time, maturation, exposure, and practice. Writing to Read is designed to improve the development of these skills and to reduce the high incidence of failure; it isn't always successful. Our research over the years indicated that we were successful in helping more than 97 percent of our children learn to write and read. Keep this fact in mind as you work with your child. Don't push, and I think you will see positive, rewarding results.

# CHAPTER 15

# WRITING TO READ AND DYSLEXIA

DYSLEXIA, THE REVERSAL or jumbling of letters and words in speech and writing which impairs the ability to read and to learn, is a problem that is said to affect 5 percent of all children and possibly as many as 15 percent. It is a problem that, more often than not, goes undiagnosed in the early years or is misdiagnosed as a form of brain damage or mental retardation. Many of these misdiagnosed children are mistakenly sent to special classes for the retarded because of their dyslexia.

We knew these facts when we began the Writing to Read experiment, and we were ready to accept the reality that the program would probably not work with these children as well as 3 to 5 percent of all other children who simply would not be able to learn with our method. We didn't intend to or try to design a system that would reduce the incidence of dyslexia in writing. We began building a structure for beginning reading on the basis of our studies of the elements of learning theory. Since there is no synthesis of these elements, no single grand design for explaining learning behavior, we tried to assemble as many of the parts as possible to make a functioning design. What we know about Writing to Read in relation to dyslexia, therefore, is very preliminary, very tentative and may well be only indicative of the potential of Writing to Read for these dyslexic children.

In our initial research population, some 900 kindergarten and first grade children, black and white, middle-class and poor, we anticipated that 5 to 15 percent would be undiagnosed handicapped children, a few with dyslexic tendencies. As we began, we quickly became aware of single-letter reversals among a few of the participants. For example, we saw children writing "fihs" for *fish* and "god" for *dog,* but we made no formal effort to correct these simple calligraphic errors. Our staff assumed that most of these children reversed letters because of their natural struggle with finger and muscle coordination. We did note, however, that a few children seemed to regress to this dyslexic condition when they were emotionally upset. When from time to time we received a child with a tear-stained face, clearly under stress, we found that the child might well mix the letters in a word despite the fact that the day before he had spelled the word correctly. We did not do much with these observations except to note them because they were outside our area of immediate interest.

But the Writing to Read System placed extra emphasis on teaching children to write. We used the encoding process of writing rather than the decoding process of reading because it enabled us to use a child's thinking power from the start. Helping children understand the principle of the alphabet transcended other concerns. The thrust of our design was to have children hear their own speech—listen to the words they were saying, hear the sounds, however they were enunciated in a spoken word, and then begin to grasp that letters were symbols for those sounds. Speaking a word and hearing its sequence of sounds was supposed to become linked eventually in the child's mind. We wanted to sharpen their ears, to turn "donwanna" into "I don't want to," not with the intent of duplicating standard English but so they could hear the word content of their own speech. Therefore, children who spoke with a Southern lilt or who used Black English were not corrected but encouraged to hear their words as they pronounced them and to begin the process of using letter symbols for the sounds to encode their speech.

What were the results? In our precomputer days the median reading scores of children in the program rose more than 25 percentile points over the previous history of the school where we were working. Equally important, and totally unanticipated, was the realization that at the close of each year, we apparently had *no* children whose reading and writing abilities were handicapped by observable dyslexic behavior. When we converted the program to the computer, informal reports from the national sample of more than 10,000 children confirmed our first observations. These test populations were located in urban, suburban, and rural centers in ten states and the District of Columbia. Teachers reported almost no indications of dyslexia among our experimental population. But such reports should be treated with skepticism.

Our clinical testing of hearing, speech, and sight revealed the expected incidence of those physical handicaps among the original test population, but significantly, children with one or more of these physiological handicaps, including previously untested mental retardation, were also found among the successful learners in the program.

What is it in the Writing to Read System that seems to have had an effect on diminishing or eliminating the incidence of dyslexia among our successful learners? The following generalizations are an attempt to explain this result:

1. Writing as an introductory step in learning to read reduces total reliance on the eyes.
2. Listening to your own speech and encoding a single sound at a time in linear progression focuses the sounds in words *in the order they must be written.*
3. The immediate exposure of the students to the electric typewriter reduces the difficulty in forming letters, which may handicap some five-year-olds.
4. The alphabetic principle that enables children to understand and to see the twenty-six letters and their combinations makes it possible to encode and to write everything they can say in correct letter order.

Our results may eventually prove little, and no claim is being made that Writing to Read is a cure for dyslexia. Still, we think the results mean something, and certainly these very tentative findings need to be followed up with intensive and focused research. At this stage we are making no claims that Writing to Read can either prevent or cure dyslexia, only that at least some part of our current expectations of the rate of incidence of this condition may be the result of our teaching methodologies and the materials employed in those methodologies, rather than an accident of nature.

# CHAPTER 16

# THE IMPORTANCE OF LITERACY

I WOULD BE remiss if, in a book about teaching writing and reading, I didn't say something about the importance of literacy and the cost of illiteracy in our society.

The basic function of literacy is the elevation of the human being. The ability to read and write at a level that allows a person to function in daily life is an essential ingredient for survival and an essential ingredient of self-worth. One could make the case that when a person stops learning he or she begins to die. If this is true—and I think it is—then it is an unfortunate fact that some, perhaps a high percentage, of the young people in our society die at an early age, so early that they never really live.

For a child, the exclusion from the learning and living society often begins with the first academic chore imposed by the schools. That chore is learning to read. When a five- or six-year-old child runs into obstacles learning to read and when those obstacles become insurmountable, it becomes evident to that child in less than a year that there is something very wrong with him or her. The implication is that the fault lies within the child. A child may assume it is his "fault." The implication is that this inability may be due to an organic pathology, hearing or sight defects, retardation, aphasias, or undetected brain damage. It is assumed that these conditions may have some relevance to a child's problems with the initial stages of reading.

These innate handicaps may, in fact, exist in a small but significant percentage of all school children. But what the schools find difficult to accept is that 85, 90, or even 95 percent of the time, the problems children have learning to read and write are not innate but the result of what the schools do (and don't do) with and to the children.

This is by no means an indictment of teachers. Teachers are like country doctors in a way. They are not specialists or researchers, they are general practitioners. They simply transfer to their patients (the children) the degree of science that was transferred to them in their training and in their reading. There is much that can be done to improve education, but teachers can only do as well as the technical base that they have acquired. Traditionally, this has been a narrow base, historically derived, apprenticeship learned, a transfer of common wisdom from an instructor to a student, from an old hand to a younger one. The public's attitude that "anyone can teach" and that "those who can't do, teach" is, in part, indicative of the problem. The public simply does not hold the role of teacher in high esteem.

For decades now the world of teaching has been involved in a hot debate on the right way or ways to teach reading. It is still an unresolved issue, but the implications of the debate started to surface in the mid-1940s. When I returned from service in World War II and was appointed a principal in Oyster Bay, Long Island, I was confronted with what was then considered a new phenomenon, namely, boys in grades nine through twelve who couldn't read. This problem was considered a male disease then and it is still largely a problem of male children. I was finishing my doctorate at the time and was spending long hours in the library researching the subject of reading. I read the specialists—Durrell, Betts, Gates, Strang, and Witty—and I took what I could from their books and attempted to translate it into a method with which I could teach reading to these male students of mine.

To test my theories I began working with some of these nonreading boys one at a time. It would have been more expedient to work with them as a group, but because they had worked hard all their lives to conceal the fact that they couldn't read, it would have been too embarrassing and psychologically damaging to group them. I applied one set of procedures, and they didn't work. I tried others and failed, and then still others. After months I had yet to see a glimmer of response.

I went back to the library and started again. This time I found a book by Grace Fernald, *Remedial Techniques in Basic School Subjects,* that I had overlooked in my previous research. Her book proposed the use of a kinesthetic process that she had used successfully with a group of college students of superior IQ who were unable to read. Fernald had these students speak words, which she then wrote in crayon. Then she had them trace over the words with a finger. They then turned the paper over and wrote the same word on their own. I started using the Fernald method, and it worked with my students as well. Like all researchers, I quickly assumed I had the answer. But, of course, I didn't have *the* answer, only part of the answer.

Since that time in 1946, I have maintained a lifelong interest in the field of reading. When I retired in 1975, I began to assemble the contents of all my accumulated information, the fragments and pieces of research about the nature of learning, and focused on that most recalcitrant of all areas of learning, learning to read.

Talking about the basic importance of reading and its sister subject writing may seem so mundane that it almost does not warrant discussion in the intellectual and academic development of children into adults. Yet the highest rate of failure in any field of education is in reading, and not to be able to read is to be closed out of the whole academic learning process because learning is then reduced to an oral function. Historically, this has been adequate for the manual skills. Carpenters were taught as apprentices in this way, as were stonemasons and other craftsmen. Until the twentieth century, oral instruction was used in the fields of medicine and law as well. A person was apprenticed to a doctor or a lawyer, just as they would to a carpenter or plumber, and they learned the necessary skills.

The institutionalization of learning and the growth of formal schooling meant that, for efficiency if nothing else, the transmission of human knowledge and skills had to be put into books. At that point, those who could not read were closed out of most learning situations because they were not able to get the necessary information to learn. In essence, they were closed out of learning for life.

This is what has happened, and is happening, to children today. Those who cannot read after the first grade must sit and wait for the interminable tick of the clock on the wall, as minute by ever-lengthening minute drags by. They have been closed out of the books in front of them by their inability to decipher meaning from the page. Theirs is a life of torture not much different from the medieval water torture in which a single drop of water hits a prisoner's forehead every few seconds. The tick of the clock, day after day, is the equivalent of that drop of water.

The figures on the number of such locked-out children vary, but conservative estimates put the national illiteracy rate at more than 27 million adults. And even these startling figures can be deceivingly low. If for example, a school reports reading scores at the 38th percentile for that school, it may be innocently seen as only 12 percentile points lower than the national average of 50. But the reality is much worse than that, because children who read at the 38th percentile are in effect nonreaders. They score at that level, not because it indicates they can read, but because the test starts from a zero base and reading in the bottom 35 percent in this country is really not reading at all. So the failure rate in the schools runs at 30 to 40 percent, and the percentage continues to grow as children get older and are identified through testing or observation as illiterate. In fact, some members of a given high-school graduating class cannot read enough to get by in normal society. This means they cannot read job applications, driver's license forms, tax forms, applications for military service, directions on medicine bottles, and of course, newspapers and magazines.

The schools like to believe that socioeconomic reasons —poverty, disrupted neighborhoods, broken homes, high mobility, lack of a support system—are the major contributors to the dropout rate, but these reasons, as compelling as they are, are secondary to the water-drip torture of not being able to learn because you can't read. This, in the final analysis, cuts the cord between the student and the educational system.

A child who cannot get information from a textbook feels isolated and will probably be retained at least once in the early grades and maybe more than one time by eighth grade. So this young person reaches the eighth grade having sat for six hours a day, 180 days a year, for eight, nine, and ten years without being able to read and to learn. This is a fiendish torture system, because everyone needs confirmation of their own worth.

This situation results in a high cost to society. There are at least two major costs of illiteracy and they are both disastrously high. One is in dollars and the other is in the quality of life in this country. The first cost runs into billions of dollars a year through jobs that can't be won or held and the cost of the welfare system that is necessary to maintain people who can't get work. But there is work for the illiterate person, and it's sad to say that the major employer is the institution of crime. Few criminal occupations require literacy; illiteracy, therefore, is a major contributor to the astronomical crime rate for which we all pay. There is scarcely a state where the cost of housing a prisoner for a year is as low as the cost of attending Harvard for a year.

The other costs are qualitative. We don't want to talk much about the fact that illiteracy results in the emasculation of life itself. The life of the mind is not the life of the esthete alone or for those few with pretensions to intellectualism. The life of the mind is the elevation of man above the level of the beast. It is the life of the gentle person, and the learned person is the gentle person; the learned society is the elevated society. Literacy is the foundation stone of civilization. Those who are concerned with the evils of our society, with the emphasis on violence and sexuality and drugs, should well concern themselves with the question of literacy at the same time.

This percentage of nonreaders today may, in reality, not be much higher than it was fifty years ago. But society has changed. The social setting in which illiteracy existed was more supportive then than now. In the pre- and postwar years many jobs that paid good wages still required only muscle. Literacy was not a prime qualification for working in mass production or smokestack industries. But as those industries have declined and the technical industries have risen, illiteracy has become a hindrance to employment, and more and more people are being excluded from that employment because they are not able to read and write.

Thus, we have a situation where reading and writing are not being taught adequately in the schools, and we have the dropout and illiteracy rate to prove it. We have a high crime rate that, at least in part, is clearly the result of the inability of a substantial portion of the population to read and write. We have people who can't get jobs and therefore don't pay taxes. And we have people who have lost that vital degree of self-worth that makes it possible to live a useful, productive, and happy life.

What are the answers? There has been no dearth of literacy programs in the last three decades, and though many millions of dollars have been spent, there have been no major breakthroughs. Some programs have achieved varying degrees of success, but the most promising efforts have been conducted on a one-to-one basis. This is the problem. There simply isn't enough money and there are not enough teachers to make any demonstrable progress if the functionally illiterate are to be taught one-on-one.

A mountain of teaching material—books, comics, films, film strips, records, video and audio tapes—have been produced over the years but none of them have hit the mark with a cross section of people who need to learn. The public eye has again focused on this problem, as it does periodically, and the media have devoted time and space to commentary and taken positive editorial positions on the subject. The time is again ripe for an all-out attack on the problem, for the development of new learning materials and the training of personnel to use them. Writing to Read is a major effort to stop the problem at its source. We can hope that this time something concrete and long-range will be done and that we are able to enlarge our literate population to a level which matches that of the other major industrialized countries of the world.